E.xx.4.81

OXFORD THEOLOGICAL MONOGRAPHS

Oxford Theological Monographs

———

THE NEW TEMPLE
The Church in the New Testament
By R. J. MCKELVEY. 1968

NEW LITURGICAL FEASTS IN LATER
MEDIEVAL ENGLAND
By R. W. PFAFF. 1970

THE LEONINE SACRAMENTARY
By D. M. HOPE. 1970

CLEMENT OF ALEXANDRIA'S TREATMENT OF
THE PROBLEM OF EVIL
By W. S. G. FLOYD. 1971

CLEMENT OF ALEXANDRIA: A STUDY IN
CHRISTIAN PLATONISM AND GNOSTICISM
By S. LILLA. 1971

THE ENGLISH SEPARATIST TRADITION
By B. R. WHITE. 1971

ANCIENT RHETORIC AND THE
ART OF TERTULLIAN
By R. D. SIDER. 1971

THE PRINCIPLE OF RESERVE IN THE WRITINGS OF JOHN HENRY CARDINAL NEWMAN

BY

ROBIN C. SELBY

OXFORD UNIVERSITY PRESS
1975

Oxford University Press, Ely House, London W. 1

GLASGOW   NEW YORK   TORONTO   MELBOURNE   WELLINGTON
CAPE TOWN   IBADAN   NAIROBI   DAR ES SALAAM   LUSAKA   ADDIS ABABA
DELHI   BOMBAY   CALCUTTA   MADRAS   KARACHI   LAHORE   DACCA
KUALA LUMPUR   SINGAPORE   HONG KONG   TOKYO

ISBN 0 19 826711 8

© *Oxford University Press 1975*

Printed in Great Britain
by Billing & Sons Limited, Guildford and London

TO
MY FAMILY

ACKNOWLEDGEMENTS

I⊤ is pleasant to record my obligations, which although not numerous, still are weighty. I owe thanks first to the Fathers of the Birmingham Oratory, for their hospitality and for the facilities which were afforded me; next, to Father Stephen Dessain for his unstinted help and active encouragement, and for his permission to quote from the rich seams of unpublished material at the Oratory.

Finally, I owe thanks to Dr. Geoffrey Rowell, whose guidance has been invaluable.

CONTENTS

ABBREVIATIONS

Apo.	*Apologia pro Vita Sua*
Ari.	*The Arians of the Fourth Century*
A. W.	*Autobiographical Writings,* ed. by Henry Tristram
Dev.	*An Essay on the Development of Christian Doctrine*
Diff. i, ii	*Certain Difficulties felt by Anglicans in Catholic Teaching*
Ess. i, ii	*Essays Critical and Historical*
G.A.	*An Essay in Aid of a Grammar of Assent*
H.S. i, ii, iii	*Historical Sketches*
K.C.	*Correspondence of John Henry Newman with John Keble and Others, 1839–45,* ed. at the Birmingham Oratory
L. and D.	*The Letters and Diaries of John Henry Newman,* ed. by C. S. Dessain
Moz. i, ii	*Letters and Correspondence of John Henry Newman during his Life in the English Church,* ed. by Anne Mozley
P.S. i–viii	*Parochial and Plain Sermons*
Prepos.	*Lectures on the Present Position of Catholics in England*
S.D.	*Sermons bearing on Subjects of the Day*
U.S.	*Fifteen Sermons preached before the University of Oxford*
V.M. i, ii	*The Via Media of the Anglican Church*
Ward. i, ii	*The Life of John Henry Cardinal Newman,* by Wilfrid Ward

The date on which a sermon was first preached is printed at the end of the quotation or in the footnote.

INTRODUCTION

THE reader who approaches Newman by way of the *Apologia* will perhaps have his curiosity roused by the use of the word 'economy'. And as he progresses in his study of Newman, he will find that the phenomena of withholding and gradual dispensation confront him on every side; this is the principle of reserve, a principle not of concealment, but of sensitivity. So striking is the way in which it manifests itself in Newman's works that Bremond 'would advise somebody to read Newman from one end to the other, for the sole purpose of extracting from his works a literary and religious manual of "economy" '.[1]

The principle of reserve links up all that is of the first importance in Newman's life and ideas; it is a sort of universal influence, which time and time again is to be discerned in his thought.

If we see a phenomenon constantly recurring in a man's life, then we conclude that this demands investigation, and that it might provide a key with which to elucidate his actions. In the same way, the principle of reserve is helpful in making out something of the workings of Newman's mind.

But however fruitful we may find reserve in our attempts to capture the elusive movement of the mind, it has more importance even than this. If the principle is truly universal, indeed, an inevitable consequence of the difficulty with which one mind communicates with another, and if it is applicable to a vast number of situations, then it is clear that we have at hand something which can tidy things up, or, as Keble would have put it, make things square. We may claim, then, that the principle helps us to see a little further into a great mind, and that it gives us some insight into one aspect of human conduct.

The method which has been adopted involves the extensive use of quotation. This approach is particularly suitable, both for the type of study, and for the subject of the study; reserve sometimes makes itself known merely by the choice of

[1] H. Bremond, *The Mystery of Newman*, tr. by H. C. Corrance, London, 1907, p. 6.

words, and the same words must be used if it is not to be lost. Moreover, Newman lends himself to quotation; he is exceptionally explicit, and can safely be left to speak for himself. It is necessary only to direct the reader's attention to the various topics. Of all those who have written on Newman, it is remarkable that few have been able to resist the temptation to quote from him at length.

CHAPTER ONE

I. THE IMPLICATIONS OF GOD'S TRANSCENDENCE — CLEMENT AND ORIGEN

WHEN Newman and the Tractarians say that God hides Himself, it is because they stand in a larger religious and philosophical tradition which lays stress on His hiddenness and total otherness, His infinite distance from our finite selves. Scripturally, the religious tradition is expressed by the exclamation 'Verily thou art a God that hidest thyself',[1] and this state is graphically described in Job: 'Behold, I go forward, but he is not there; and backward, but I cannot perceive him: On the left hand, where he doth work, but I cannot behold him: he hideth himself on the right hand, that I cannot see him.'[2] If God is totally other, He can only be represented analogically, and we are at once confronted with the impossibility of knowing Him. Further, His hiddenness has immediate doctrinal implications, which for Newman are as follows: 'I can only answer, that either there is no Creator, or this living society of men is in a true sense discarded from His presence.'[3]

The philosophical tradition is derived from Plato, and consists of an attempt to express the concept of God: to find what is meant by the word 'God', and what can logically be expressed by the word; to see what it includes, and what it excludes. The argument runs thus: God must be one, for otherwise we would have to speak of Gods instead of God; the idea of God demands that He be Omnipotent, Omniscient, Infinite, Eternal, and therefore completely outside time and space, for His presence must not be limited in any way to one moment or place. This idea of God excludes action, for since God is good, He can only act to achieve a greater good, which manifestly involves an absurdity.

---

[1] Isaiah 45: 15.   [2] Job 23: 8, 9.
[3] *Apologia pro Vita Sua*, ed. by M. J. Svaglic, Oxford, 1967, p. 217.

The difficulty of grasping the idea of God shows us that it is beyond the capability of our minds; it emphasizes that we are finite, and that He is infinite, and therefore incomprehensible to us. Described thus, God is a Platonic Absolute, an Idea, and the nearest notion we can obtain is that expressed by Newman in the *Arians*, of 'everlasting and unchangeable quiescence';[4] God is in a state of being, while man is always changing, and therefore in a state of becoming. The question then arises, what possible connection can there be between this transcendent God and the material world? The answer is given that there is an intermediary, the Logos, through whom the world is brought into existence.

Hence there is a close similarity between the Scriptural and philosophical accounts of God, and the early Fathers were quick to assimilate the Platonic reasonings into their system, arguing that Plato had in fact plagiarized them from Moses.

It is worth remarking that the Tractarians held that God could be known in a variety of ways—through His Son, His Church, the Sacraments, the creation, the conscience, and, for those who were highly favoured, through Christ's Indwelling. Moreover, God's hand could be discerned in the workings of Providence, the types and symbols which shadowed Him forth, and through His inspired Scriptures. But the idea of God which we are considering sets aside all of these, and is intent only on seeing the conditions under which God communicates to His creatures. There are several points to note here: that He is hidden from us; that any communication of Himself to us must be imperfect, since we are incapable of comprehending it; that, even while He reveals Himself to us, He is hiding, since we are on trial in our present state, and must not have things made too easy for us.

With this particular idea of God in mind, we now turn to the Fathers from whom Newman gained the ideas of reserve and economy which he expounded in the *Arians of the Fourth Century*: in the *Apologia* he wrote:

> The broad philosophy of Clement and Origen carried me away; the philosophy, not the theological doctrine;

4 *The Arians of the Fourth Century*, London, 1876, p. 75.

. . . some portions of their teaching, magnificent in themselves, came like music to my inward ear, as if the response
to ideas, which, with little external to encourage them, I
had cherished so long. These were based on the mystical
or sacramental principle, and spoke of the various
Economies or Dispensations of the Eternal. (*Apo.* 36)

Since God is incomprehensible, revealed only through the
Logos, Clement tells us that the Ruler of All is a Being difficult
to grasp and apprehend, 'ever receding and withdrawing from
him who pursues. But He who is far off has—oh ineffable
marvel!—come very near. . . . It is clear, then, that the truth
has been hidden from us.'[5]

The prophets, Scripture, and Christ each bring the truth
before us in a way suited to our faculties: 'For the Divine
Being cannot be declared as it exists: but as we who are
fettered in the flesh were able to listen, so the prophets spake
to us; the Lord savingly accommodating Himself to the
weakness of men.'[6]

But although truth is adapted, as a matter of expedience,
to our abilities, this disclosure of truth is still strictly
guarded and limited: Christ 'did not certainly disclose to
the many what did not belong to the many; but to the few
to whom He knew that they belonged, who were capable of
receiving and being moulded according to them. But secret
things are entrusted to speech, not to writing, as is the case
with God.'[7] Equally, Scripture cloaks its meaning in enigmas
and parables so that we shall become more inquisitive and
watchful for salvation.[8]

Clement himself wrote unsystematically, using enigmatic
language lest his readers should understand him in a wrong
sense, and to ensure that anyone wishing to inquire further
would have to avail himself of an instructor:

For I do not mention that the *Miscellanies* [*Stromateis*],
forming a body of varied erudition, wish artfully to conceal
the seeds of knowledge. As, then, he who is fond of hunting
captures the game after seeking, tracking, scenting, hunting

---

[5] *The Writings of Clement of Alexandria*, tr. by W. Wilson, Edinburgh, 1867, 1869,
Stromateis, ii. 4.
[6] Ibid. ii. 44.   [7] Ibid. i. 356.   [8] Ibid. ii. 378.

it down with dogs; so truth, when sought and got with toil, appears a delicious thing. Why, then, you will ask, did you think it fit that such an arrangement should be adopted in your memoranda? Because there is great danger in divulging the secret of the true philosophy to those, whose delight it is unsparingly to speak against everything, not justly; and who shout forth all kinds of names and words indecorously, deceiving themselves and beguiling those who adhere to them. (*Stromateis*, Wilson, i. 361)

In the fifth part of the *Stromateis*, Clement gives four reasons why symbols are used; first, so that unworthy people will be excluded; second, because interpreters would be needed, so that the Apostolic tradition would be handed on faithfully. In this way, 'receiving truth at the hands of those who knew it well, we would be more earnest and less liable to deception, and those worthy of them would profit.'[9] Third, when truth is veiled, it is more suggestive, and makes a greater impression on the recipient; and finally, symbols have several meanings, which will be apprehended by the Gnostic, but by none less worthy. By his use of the word 'Gnostic', Clement boldly asserts that Christianity has advanced to such a degree that there is a Christian Gnosticism which cannot be mistaken for the Gnostic mystery-religions. Further, this word is used to make much the same sort of distinction found in the fourth Gospel, between those who see without knowing, and those who see and believe.

Who, then, is the favoured man who is a Gnostic? He is the person who searches for truth in the right way, who alone is able to understand and explain the things spoken by the Spirit obscurely,[10] and whose gnostic ability has three effects: the knowledge of things, the performance of whatever the Word suggests, and the capability of delivering, in a way suitable to God, the secrets veiled in the truth.[11]

The vexed question here is whether the Gnostic has, so to speak, an unfair advantage over simpler folk, and certainly Clement's four categories of conversion seem to countenance this notion. Using an ingenious figure drawn from grafting, Clement tells us that there are plain people belonging to

---

[9] Ibid. ii. 254.   [10] Ibid. ii. 372.   [11] Ibid. ii. 408.

the Gentiles, who receive the word superficially. Next, there are those who have studied philosophy, and once their dogmas are cut through, they acknowledge the truth. 'The third mode of engrafting applies to rustics and heretics, who are brought by force to the truth.'[12] The fourth graft is where the bud is kept uninjured: 'This is the style of gnostic teaching, which is capable of looking into things themselves. This mode is, in truth, of most service in the case of cultivated trees.'[13]

But although this seems to make gnostic ability a matter of education and intellect, Clement elsewhere lays great stress on the need for preparation and instruction: '*The Instructor* . . . has already exhibited the training and nurture up from the state of childhood, that is, the course of life which from elementary instruction grows by faith; and in the case of those enrolled in the number of men, prepares beforehand the soul, endued with virtue, for the reception of gnostic knowledge.'[14] There is some obscurity here, but it seems plain that one can grow towards gnostic knowledge. Thus when Clement tells us that 'the apostle, then, manifestly announces a double faith, or rather one which admits of growth and perfection; for the common faith lies beneath as a foundation',[15] he may mean no more than that a man is a gnostic because he has grown in faith, rather than he is a man whose gnosticism has enabled him to grow in faith.

Origen speaks in very similar terms to Clement, although his emphasis and intentions are rather different. For him, too, God is hidden: 'let us grant that *God is hard to perceive.* Yet He is not the only being hard for a person to perceive. For the divine Logos is hard to perceive; and the same is true of the wisdom in which God has made all things.'[16] Origen uses an idea of Irenaeus to explain the need for a gradual communication of truth; God wanted men to know the mysteries from the beginning, but could only communicate as much as they were able to bear.[17] Hence accommodations are made to our frailty; the Prophets 'said without any obscurity whatever could be at once understood as beneficial to their

[12] Ibid. ii. 373.   [13] Ibid. ii. 374.   [14] Ibid. ii. 302.   [15] Ibid. ii. 221.
[16] Origen, *Contra Celsum*, tr. by H. Chadwick, Cambridge, 1953, p. 383.
[17] Jean Daniélou, *Origen*, tr. by W. Mitchell, London, 1955, p. 118.

hearers and helpful towards attaining moral reformation',[18] but concealed mysterious and esoteric truths in parables and proverbs, so that those who attained the further truths would be worthy of them. Equally, Jesus 'always expressed Himself in language appropriate to his hearers',[19] and after His Passion, He 'with deliberate care measured out to each individual that which was right'.[20] Even His appearance 'was not just the same to those who saw him, but varied according to their individual capacity'.[21] This method was necessary because even the disciples were 'still beginners and immature',[22] and because He saw 'that it is very difficult to eradicate from a soul doctrines with which he was almost born, and was brought up until he reached man's estate'.[23]

In this way Origen draws out the idea that truth is relative, and that the doctrines of hell and eternal punishment are only necessary for the multitude. Hence the Logos accommodates Himself to the masses who read the Bible, and wisely utters threatening words with a hidden meaning:

> Probably, just as some words are suitable for use with children and are appropriate for their tender age, in order to exhort them to be better . . . the ordinary interpretation of punishments is suitable because they have not the capacity for any other means of conversion and of repentance from many evils, except that of fear and the suggestion of punishment. (*Contra Celsum*, Chadwick, p. 276)

Further, Origen tells us that 'there was no need for the multitude that the words put into God's mouth, which were intended to be addressed to them, should correspond to His real character'.[24]

So far, we note a rather arbitrary distinction between the intelligent and the multitude, and a ready assumption that hell and punishment are not real things but only convenient means of scaring the unintelligent into goodness. However, Origen appears to have found himself in something of a dilemma when Celsus argued first, that Christianity was only for the unintelligent, and second, that it possessed esoteric

---

[18] *Contra Celsum*, Chadwick, p. 403.   [19] Ibid., p. 97.   [20] Ibid., p. 117.
[21] Ibid., p. 115.   [22] Ibid., p. 101.   [23] Ibid., p. 68.   [24] Ibid., p. 240.

doctrines which were withheld from the uninitiated. Origen's answer therefore seems inconsistent, since it faces attacks from two directions. On the one hand he maintains that 'the gospel so desires wise men among believers that, in order to exercise the understanding of the hearers, it has expressed certain truths in enigmatic forms . . .'[25] He frequently seems to prefer intelligent men to the multitude:

> For we do everything in our power to see that our gathering consists of intelligent men, and we do dare to bring forward in the common discourse at the time of our gathering our most noble and divine beliefs when we have an intelligent audience. But we conceal and pass over the more profound truths whenever we see that the meeting consists of simple-minded folk who are in need of teaching which is figuratively called milk. (*Contra Celsum*, Chadwick, p. 164)

At another time he retorts to Celsus that 'if by "stupid" you mean those who are not clever but very superstitious, I answer you that I do all in my power to improve even these, but I certainly do not want the assembly of Christians to consist of these. I seek rather the cleverer and sharper minds because they are able to understand the explanation of problems and of the hidden truths set forth in the law, the prophets, and the gospels.'[26] We gather here that Origen wishes to confine Christianity to the intelligent, while grudgingly admitting the existence of the multitude. Yet, on the other hand, while he still allows that 'to have been educated, and to have studied the best doctrines, and to be intelligent, does not hinder us from knowing God, but helps us'[27] he also maintains that Christianity is as much for the simpler folk as for the intelligent. Thus Christ uses Hebrew because it is understood by more people:

> the divine nature, which cares not only for those supposed to have been educated in Greek learning but also for the rest of mankind, came down to the level of the ignorant multitude of hearers, that by using the style familiar to them it might encourage the mass of the common people to listen. After they have once been introduced to Christianity

they are easily able to aspire to grasp even deeper truths
which are concealed in the Bible. (*Contra Celsum*, Chadwick,
p. 445)

In this way Origen is able to open Christianity to all, so
long as they are initiated in the right, catechetical way:

> We say that it is the task of those who teach the true doc-
> trines to help as many people as they can, and as far as it is
> in their power to win everyone over to the truth by their
> love to mankind—not only the unintelligent, but also
> the stupid, and again not just the Greeks without including
> the barbarians as well.
> —For our prophets, and Jesus and his apostles, were
> careful to use a method of teaching which not only contains
> the truth but is also able to win over the multitude. After
> conversion and entrance into the Church each individual
> according to his capacity can ascend to the hidden truths
> in the words which seem to have a mean style. (*Contra
> Celsum*, Chadwick, p. 316)

The catechumen is therefore led towards the truth, step by
step:

> . . . we put the gospel before each man in a form suited to
> his character and condition, for we have learnt to 'know
> how we ought to answer each individual.' There are some
> people to whom we preach only an exhortation to believe,
> since they are incapable of anything more; but with others
> we do all we can to approach them with rational arguments
> 'by questions and answers'. (*Contra Celsum*, Chadwick, p. 324)

It follows therefore that there are three degrees of understanding; divine wisdom, knowledge, and faith, 'since salvation must be available also for the simple folk who advance in
religion as far as they can comprehend'.[28]

This line of thought leads us to inquire precisely what
status 'faith' has, since it is the portion of the simpler folk.
Clearly it is something less than wisdom, but is it a second best
for all that? Origen answers this question when he says:
'As this matter of faith is so much talked of, I have to reply

---

[28] Ibid., p. 327.

that we accept it as useful for the multitude, and that we admittedly teach those who cannot abandon everything and pursue a study of rational argument to believe without thinking out their reasons.'[29] Again, he tells us that 'the simple-minded masses, however, who cannot comprehend the complex theology of the wisdom of God, must trust themselves to God and to the Saviour of our race, and be content simply with the *ipse dixit* of Jesus rather than with anything beyond this'.[30]

There seems little doubt in all this that Origen prefers the intelligent to the multitude, and that those who are only capable of faith come off a mere second best. This distinction may explain why Newman is careful to point out in the passage already quoted that he was carried away by the philosophy rather than by the theological doctrines.

If we may venture upon a parallel, we might say that Newman is Origen to Keble's Clement; Origen is similar to Newman in his controversial ability, his willingness to use an *argumentum ad hominem*, while his use of reserve is widely varied. Clement's handling of reserve, however, merely reflects traditional usage. We might hazard, too, that Newman was more sympathetic to Origen than he was to Clement; the idea that an economy is the nearest approach we can make to truth, compatible with our condition, is found frequently in Newman's writings, and we may conjecture that when he expressed his notorious maxim that it is no more than a hyperbole to say that a lie is the nearest thing to the truth,[31] he may have had in mind this sentence of Origen's:

> Do you not say, Celsus, that sometimes it is allowable to use deceit and lying as a medicine? Why, then, is it unthinkable that something of this sort occurred with the purpose of bringing salvation? For some characters are reformed by certain doctrines which are more false than true, just as physicians sometimes use similar words to their patients. (*Contra Celsum*, Chadwick, p. 196)

We have said enough in this section to show that Newman would have found a good deal about the communication of

[29] Ibid., p. 13.   [30] Ibid., p. 190.
[31] *Fifteen Sermons preached before the University of Oxford*, London, 1872, p. 341 n: 2 February 1843.

religious truth and economical representation in the two
Fathers he especially singles out. When he came to read them,
he found that the ideas they express chimed in remarkably
with what he had previously felt. It is now time to look at the
development of his mind before he knew that the principle of
reserve was sanctioned by antiquity.

ii. NEWMAN'S EARLY DEVELOPMENT

There are some difficulties about the appearance of the
principle of reserve in Newman's writings. The first resolves
itself into a question of whether reserve was natural to him or
not, and if so, how it was compatible with his Evangelicalism,
since the emotions and the methods of the Evangelicals are
remote from the practice of reserve. And if reserve was not
natural, but something he 'acquired', how did it emerge
through his Evangelicalism? Another difficulty arises; in
Newman's writings, reserve manifests itself in a bewildering
variety of guises. Is it possible to detect the very first appearance it makes, with the material available to us, and can we
see what form it takes as its vehicle?

With these questions in mind, then, the position I would
like to maintain is this: from his earliest years Newman felt
that if there was a God, He must be hidden and infinitely
different from ourselves. This is confirmed by a revealing comment on Pusey:

> It suggests another thought, which is brought home to me
> again and again. He does not hold the utter, infinite separa-
> tion between the Creator and the creature; but, like the
> elder brother in the Parable, or the Pharisee, thinks that
> we have claims on God, and are something more than what
> grace makes us. I suspect this is at the bottom of a vast
> deal of Puseyism. It is a curious fact that my original
> Evangelical–Calvinistic bias has kept me personally (what-
> ever I may have *written*) from feeling the force of this
> temptation. . . .[32]

[32] *The Letters and Diaries of John Henry Newman*, ed. by C. S. Dessain, Oxford, 1961– ,
xiv. 235.

Newman was conscious that he was an Evangelical, and that he held what Evangelicals held. Thus in one of his first conversations with Pusey, Newman fears that Pusey 'is prejudiced against Thy children', even though he is delighted with Pusey's 'seriousness'.[33] He terms himself an Evangelical, and places himself under their banner. But at the same time, he was aware that he did not feel what Evangelicals were meant to feel, however much he might believe as they believed, and so in his Journal for June or July 1821 he writes: 'I speak of (the process of) conversion with great diffidence, being obliged to adopt the language of books. For my own feelings, as far as I remember, were so different from any account I have ever read, that I dare not go by what *may* be an individual case.'[34] Moreover, he often laments his coldness, and it is not improbable that he has in mind the emotions which Evangelicals were meant to feel, and which he was only too conscious that, though a professed Evangelical, he did *not* feel: 'I can read religious books, the most spiritual, with great pleasure, and, when so engaged, feel myself warmed to prayer and thanks giving; but let the appointed hour of devotion arrive, and I am cold and dead.'[35] The distinction between what he believes and what he himself feels is made with particular clarity in this passage of 1 June 1821:

> When I have heard or read that Horsley, Milner &c were adverse to the introduction of the doctrines of election, final perseverance &c into the pulpit, I have wondered at and been sorry for such an opinion. However, when I come to examine my own ideas on the subject, I have much the same sentiments. Do we see St Paul or St Peter in the Acts addressing the unconverted in this manner? (*A.W.* 166)

As an Evangelical, he knew he should have approved of such doctrines being preached; as J. H. Newman, he knew that he did not. This situation, in which Evangelical beliefs temporarily overlay and obscured his own feelings, without being nourished by true Evangelical feelings, could only continue for as long as it was left untried. The test came when Newman

---

[33] *Autobiographical Writings*, ed. by H. Tristram, London, 1956, pp. 190 f.
[34] Ibid., p. 166.   [35] Ibid., p. 165.

was ordained and when shortly he would have to preach, and
to decide whether he would preach in the characteristically
Evangelical way, or otherwise.

We have already seen that he was aware that there was a
particularly Evangelical way of preaching and manner of
behaving. Now the question arose, whether he should adopt
them. Presumably, if he had been questioned on this subject
before, he would have answered that he had not thought about
it, but supposed that he would use Evangelical methods. However, during the Long Vacation of 1824, Newman spent a
good deal of his time in the company of Edward Hawkins:
'when the other Fellows were away, they two had Hall and
Common Room to themselves. They dined and read the
Papers, they took their evening walk, and then their tea, in
company; and, while Mr. Newman was full of the difficulties
of a young curate, he found in Mr. Hawkins a kind and able
adviser.'[36] Hawkins's own opinions on preaching are sufficiently indicated by a quotation from his sermon recommend-
ing systematic preaching, delivered in St. Mary's in 1825,
when he asks: 'Is it meant then that all the high truths of
the Gospel are to be taught to all persons at all times, and at
all hazards? Certainly not. To teach Christianity with integ-
rity, is not to teach it without discretion.'[37] Hawkins gave
him J. B. Sumner's *Apostolical Preaching*, and argued with him
on the basis of this book. In later life, Newman said that Sumner
wrote it against Evangelical Preaching, and both in the
Apologia[38] and in his *Autobiographical Writings*, Newman recorded that this work had a considerable effect on him:

> . . . Criticism such as this, which of course he did not deliver
> once for all, but as occasions offered, and which, when New-
> man dissented, he maintained and enforced, had a great
> though a gradual effect upon the latter, when carefully
> studied in the work from which it was derived, and which
> Hawkins gave him; this was Sumner's *Apostolical Preaching*.
> This book was successful in the event beyond anything else,

[36] Ibid., p. 77.
[37] Edward Hawkins, *Systematic Preaching recommended in a Sermon preached June 4,
1825, in the Church of St. Mary the Virgin, Oxford*, Oxford, 1825, p. 6.
[38] *Apo.* 21.

in routing out evangelical doctrines from Mr. Newman's Creed. (*A.W.* 77)

Thus it is most interesting to remark that Sumner's book recommends reserve, though without using the word. He points out that religion has its 'vestibule' and its 'inmost recesses'.[39] Further, he observes that 'two congregations can scarcely be found in precisely the same state of religious knowledge and advancement, or with the same capabilities of comprehending a method of treating a subject'.[40] Therefore it is the preacher's duty to discriminate:

> He will not dwell at length upon what is called Christian liberty, to a congregation which is seeking a cloak for sin; nor abound in strong and unguarded statements upon those points which are liable to be wrested to the destruction of the hearer, till he is assured his flock are able 'to bear them'. (*Apostolical Preaching*, p. 12)

Sumner makes the distinction which Thomas Mozley was later to make in an article upon reserve in the *British Critic*, between 'field preaching' and 'church preaching';[41] that is, between preaching which aims to stir up emotion, since there is only one opportunity to bring about conversions, and between careful preaching to those who are under the constant supervision of the preacher.[42]

Later on in the book, Sumner rejects violent invectives on human nature in general, admitting that the method does work on the lower classes, but arguing that they usually are gross sinners anyway, and feel a pleasure at seeing their superiors brought down to the same level as themselves, which should be discouraged. Instead, he believes that

> The considerate minister will not court such dangerous applause: there is no edification communicated by exciting feelings of disgust on one side, and of malignant exultation

[39] J. B. Sumner, *Apostolical Preaching considered in an Examination of St. Paul's Epistles*, London, 1815, p. 5. Henceforward abbreviated as *Apostolical Preaching*.
[40] Ibid., p. 10.
[41] *British Critic and Quarterly Theological Review*, vol. xxxi, no. 61, 1842, p. 219.
[42] *Apostolical Preaching*, p. 25.

on the other. St. Paul was aware that it was safer to persuade than to repel; and knew that even the passions and
prejudices of the mind may become powerful auxiliaries
to the work of grace, when rightly touched and skilfully
handled. (*Apostolical Preaching*, p. 115)

Sumner goes on to point out that at Athens, St. Paul did not
'break out into passionate exclamations against the impurity
and senselessness of heathen idolatry', but instead employs
economy, and 'takes advantage of a circumstance in that very
idolatry, to bring over the minds of the people to the truth
he came to deliver'.[43] Sumner urges the preacher not to be
content with retaining one class only of his congregation, but
to conciliate all sections of it. He considers that it is not so
much *what* is preached, as the *manner* in which it is preached,
that is important: 'The spirit of these remarks is applicable to
other doctrines. Many preachers take to themselves the satisfaction expressed by St Paul, that he "had not shunned to
declare the whole counsel of God", whose *manner* of declaring
it bears very little resemblance to that of the Apostle.'[44]
Later he comments on St. Paul's conformity to the Jewish
ceremonies while at Jerusalem, and suggests that 'complaisance
and candour was more likely to forward the cause of Christ,
than unauthorized scruples or inflexible austerity'.[45]

In all these extracts, it is noticeable that Sumner employs
the language of reserve, and that he recommends discrimination in preaching, to avert the danger of communicating religious knowledge to those who are not ready for it.

It is probable, then, that this book, together with his
conversations with Hawkins, helped to lay bare his own feelings; that here is the issue which provided a form wherein
Newman might see his inner mind manifested, in such a
way as to banish the Evangelical methods of preaching. When
the question was seriously put to him, the whole bent of his
mind constrained him to answer that Evangelical preaching
was neither Apostolical, nor even recommended by common
sense or experience. For when he became curate of St. Clement's
in 1825, he found that 'the religion which he had received
from John Newton and Thomas Scott would not work in a

⁴³ Ibid., p. 116.   ⁴⁴ Ibid., p. 117.   ⁴⁵ Ibid., p. 228.

parish; that it was unreal; that this he had actually found as a fact, as Mr Hawkins had told him beforehand. . . .'[46] This passage suggests that before Newman came under Hawkins's influence, he assumed that preaching should be of the Evangelical kind, and there is evidence for this view in the following statement from the autobiographical memoir: 'Up to this time the latter [i.e. Newman] took for granted, if not intelligently held, the opinions called evangelical. . . .'[47] When he came to write this memoir and to look back on his youth, he found that Evangelical ways of thought had been powerless to induce Evangelical feelings or behaviour in him:

> . . . the critical peculiarities of evangelical religion had never been congenial to him, though he had fancied he held them. Its emotional and feverish devotion and its tumultuous experiences were foreign to his nature, which indeed was ever conspicuously faulty in the opposite direction, as being in a way incapable, as if physically, of enthusiasm, however legitimate and guarded. (*A.W.* 82)

This line of thought leads us to a note which he made while on retreat in Rome in 8–17 April 1847. It is a point which he makes several times during his life, and to which we shall return in a later chapter.[48] But here he gives it a direction which is most apposite:

> It is difficult to explain and strange even to myself, but I have this peculiarity, that in the movement of my affections, whether sacred or human, my physical strength cannot go beyond certain limits. I am always languid in the contemplation of divine things, like a man walking with his feet bound together. I am held as it were by a fetter, by a sort of physical law, so that I cannot be forcible in preaching and speaking, nor fervent in praying and meditating. (*A.W.* 248)

[46] *A.W.* 79.   [47] Ibid., p. 77.
[48] Cf. *L. and D.* xv. 242: 'All my life I have complained of ἀδυναμία [powerlessness], as I have called it. I mean a strange imprisonment, as if a chain were round my limbs and my faculties, hindering me doing more than a certain maximum—a sort of moral tether.' This passage is discussed in greater detail on p. 98.

Not only was Newman unfitted for fervent displays in the
pulpit through the weakness of his voice,[49] to which he refers
many times throughout his life, but he seems to have felt
himself constitutionally and providentially restrained from
plunging into an excessively emotional type of religion.

What has been said so far is the outline, which can now
be filled with some subordinate detail. In January 1817[50]
Walter Mayers, his schoolmaster and 'the human means of
this beginning of divine faith in me',[51] gave Newman Bishop
Beveridge's *Private Thoughts*. Nearly sixty years later, Newman
wrote in his copy that '. . . no book was more dear to me, or
exercised a more powerful influence over my devotion and
my habitual thoughts'.[52] In this work he would have found
a resolution to exercise wisdom and discretion, 'as in discourse,
my zeal may put me upon throwing pearls before swine, or
using words when silence may be more commendable'.[53]
On the next page, the Bishop expresses another favourite
thought of Newman's: 'that may be a good work at one
time and place which is not at another; and may be very innocent and becoming in one person, though quite contrary in
another.'[54] I do not maintain that this had any influence upon
Newman, but that it was a hint, a signpost in a certain direction. Similarly, 'the admirable works of Jones of Nayland'[55]
on Scripture would have impelled him in the same direction,
with the idea that truths in Scripture are expressed mysteriously
rather than directly.

Hawkins had another practical influence upon Newman;
in his great sermon on Tradition, which Newman heard as an
undergraduate, and studied when Hawkins later gave it to
him, he pointed out that the distribution of Bibles does not
automatically make converts: it is 'but a single link in
the chain of necessary means towards that important end.'[56]
For Newman, this struck 'at the root of the principle on which
the Bible Society was set up',[57] and on 21 February 1826

[49] *Letters and Correspondence of John Henry Newman during his Life in the English Church*,
ed. by Anne Mozley, London 1891, i. 84.
[50] *A.W.* 152.   [51] *Apo.* 17.   [52] *Apo.* 479.
[53] *The Theological Works of William Beveridge*, Oxford, 1842, viii. 259.
[54] Ibid., viii. 260.   [55] *Apo.* 18.
[56] Edward Hawkins, *A Dissertation upon the Use and Importance of Unauthoritative
Tradition*, Oxford, 1819, p. 70.   [57] *Apo.* 22.

he records: 'I have doubts about the propriety of the Bible Society.'[58] In this way the ground was cleared for the full possession of Newman's mind by the principle of reserve.

Other members of the Oriel Common Room, too, expressed opinions implying the operation of the principle of reserve. Copleston, for example, preached four discourses on the doctrines of necessity and predestination, in which he maintains that since the nature of God is incomprehensible, the attributes we ascribe to Him cannot be literally true: 'They are not to be understood then in their literal sense as *direct* and *proper* appellations; and we ought never to pursue these comparisons farther than the occasion on which they are used requires; nor draw positive conclusions from such premises as if the terms were in themselves proper and thoroughly understood.'[59] These discourses led to some controversy, and in the same year Whately defended his colleague by publishing an edition of Archbishop King's *Discourse on Predestination*, which Copleston had taken as his guide on the subject. In this work we find that passions are only ascribed to God by way of analogy, and that we have no proper notion of them, any more than a man born blind has of sight and colours, and so we cannot pretend to determine what is consistent with them: 'for this were to reason from things that are only comparatively and improperly ascribed to God, and by way of analogy and accommodation to our capacities, as if they were properly and univocally the same in him and in us.'[60] From this Newman might have drawn the beginnings of his theories of economical representation.

Again, Davison argued that there was a discernible progress in all the communications made concerning the doctrine of the Atonement, and concluded that 'whether for our own information, or for the conviction of others, it would be wise that some regard to this order should be maintained.'[61] Ideas such as the

---

[58] *A.W.* 208.

[59] Edward Copleston, *An Enquiry into the Doctrines of Necessity and Predestination. In Four Discourses preached before the University of Oxford*, London, 1821, p. 118.

[60] *The Right Method of Interpreting Scripture, in what relates to the Nature of the Deity, and His Dealings with Mankind, illustrated in a Discourse on Predestination*, by Dr. King, with notes by Richard Whately, Oxford, 1821, p. 19.

[61] *The Remains and Occasional Publications of the late Rev. John Davison*, Oxford, 1841, p. 157.

hiddenness and otherness of God, and the progressive nature of Revelation were evidently frequently expressed in the Oriel Common Room, and would have served to lead Newman in the same direction.

In 1825 he studied Butler's *Analogy*. He had read it before, in 1823, but now, since he was undertaking his curacy, it was necessary to put his ideas into systematic shape. He notes that it had 'an important indirect effect upon him in the same direction [as Sumner's *Apostolical Preaching*] as placing his doctrinal views on a broad philosophical basis, with which an emotional religion could have little sympathy'.[62] Not only did his adherence to Butler's ideas make an emotional, Evangelical type of religion impossible, but it led him to see that one should follow Butler's example and cultivate External Religion, rather than deliver doctrines over the pulpit: 'His wonderfully gifted intellect caught the idea which had actually been the rule of the Primitive Church, of teaching the more sacred truths by rites and ceremonies.'[63] His development was aided by his acquaintance and then growing friendship with Keble, in whose character reserve was prominent; Isaac Williams records how both he and Hurrell Froude were struck by Keble's habits of reserve. Doubtless, when anecdotes of Keble's conduct were related, such as the time when Keble put Law's *Serious Call to a Holy and Devout Life* into a drawer, instead of leaving it lying around where it might do good, Newman would have found them intelligible.[64] With such an example of reserve before him, Newman would have been more likely to note instances of reserve when he began to read the Fathers.

In autumn 1816 Newman read Joseph Milner's *Church History*, and was 'nothing short of enamoured of the long extracts from St. Augustine, St. Ambrose, and the other Fathers which I found there'.[65] In this work he would have found many references to the idea of reserve in communicating religious knowledge, which would have familiarized him with

---

[62] *A.W.* 78.

[63] Cambridge University Library, unpublished letter J. H. Newman to J. Stephen, 16 March 1835, Add. 7349/15(c) 138.

[64] *The Autobiography of Isaac Williams, B.D.*, ed. by the Ven. Sir George Prevost, London, 1892, p. 28.

[65] *Apo.* 20.

it, and prepared him for the fuller exposition which he found in Sumner's book.

He was still reading the Fathers in 1823, for in that year he drew up an argument for the strict observance of the Sabbath from St. John Chrysostom and others.[66] However, we do not know whether it was then or in 1828, when he first started to read the Fathers through,[67] that he found that Clement and Origen had systematically practised reserve. The later date is more probable, but at all events his history of the Arians, which he wrote before the Mediterranean trip, and which was published on 5 November 1833, shows that the idea of reserve had been entirely assimilated. By that time, all the separate influences had been brought together, and external forms had been found for that natural restraint and reserve of which he was so conscious. The way is now clear for a survey of the way in which Newman put reserve to practical use.

[66] *A.W.* 83.   [67] *Apo.* 35.

CHAPTER TWO

THE COMMUNICATION OF
RELIGIOUS TRUTH

IF it is proposed to employ reserve in the communication of religious truth, then the relationship between the people who receive the truth and the person whose responsibility it is to impart it to them will lead us to focus our attention upon his character, and his opinion of the people to whom he is communicating the truth. This chapter will therefore attempt to trace Newman's use of reserve as a method of proselytizing, and to ascertain if a change in his method was accompanied by a corresponding change in his attitude to the people.

Newman devoted a number of pages in his *Arians of the Fourth Century* to describing the system of secrecy operated by the Primitive Church. The aspects which he drew out 'with the partiality of a neophyte'[1] are divided into reserve and economy. Reserve 'may be considered as withholding the truth, and the other [i.e. economy] as setting it out to advantage'.[2] Reserve is concerned with fostering the reverence due to sacred things, by withholding them, until men are worthy to behold them. Further, reserve affords a prudent and necessary method of proselytizing, for it enables the catechist to lead the catechumen on step by step until he finds himself in possession of Divine Truth, since 'the more sublime truths of Revelation afford . . . no nourishment to the souls of the unbelieving or unstable.'[3]

While reserve safeguards sacred things by withholding them, the economical method consists of the 'accommodation to the feelings and prejudices of the hearer, in leading him to the reception of a novel or unacceptable doctrine'.[4] Newman shows clearly that both reserve and economy are susceptible of abuse, and that there is the danger of priestcraft or actual falsehood in the use of these methods.

[1] *Apo.* 36.   [2] *Ari.* 65.   [3] *Ari.* 44.   [4] *Ari.* 71.

Until the beginning of the Oxford Movement, Newman was more interested in reserve than economy; he found reserve of practical assistance in his parochial work, or in his preaching, but for the moment he could find no employment for economy. This distinction is clearly made in a correspondence which took place shortly after the publication of his first volume of *Parochial Sermons* in March 1834 between himself, Samuel Wilberforce, and James Stephen, in which Newman defended his sermons from charges made by Wilberforce. It is plain that at this stage Newman has no idea that the time is not far off when he will have to employ all the methods of the Primitive Church in order to lead his unwilling hearers on into the possession of the complete truth, for he writes:

Of course after all one must go by one's own judgment—and I may account that to be indulgence to the evil principles of the age which another may consider a necessary and prudent accommodation. Again I am persuaded that often, when one accommodates the age, one hurts posterity. What is the reason that this or that man's works are brought to countenance errors now extinct, except that he has yielded to the superstitions or fancies of his own time?—in consequence what in him was an economy is taken as his authority in favor of some mistaken view.[5]

He is evidently more alive to the dangers than to the advantages of economy. But in the same correspondence he describes the faults of Evangelistic preaching, and sets out his own ideas, which depend upon the principle of reserve. He feels that Wilberforce is asking him to 'lug in' the doctrine of the Holy Spirit, and replies: 'I will never be so irreverent as to (if I may so say) lug in any doctrine, much less so sacred a one. The Peculiars can never say a thing in a natural way. . . . I assure you, the received way of introducing the H.S. is to my feelings *shocking*.'[6] Wilberforce had been forwarding copies of the correspondence to James Stephen, whose father

[5] Bodleian Library, Wilberforce Papers, C5, J. H. Newman to S. Wilberforce, 10 November 1834, p. 7. The whole correspondence has been summarized by David Newsome, 'Justification and Sanctification: Newman and the Evangelicals', *Journal of Theological Studies*, New Series, vol. xv, 1964, pp. 37 ff.

[6] Wilberforce Papers, C5, 4 February 1835, p. 22.

had been a friend of William Wilberforce and a member of the Clapham sect, and from whom he derived the purest evangelical doctrines. Stephen was shocked to find that Wilberforce had sent a critique of the sermons, written by him, to Newman, and wrote to apologize, whereupon a correspondence began between him and Newman. In a most important letter of 16 March 1835 Newman gives his opinion that too much is expected of a sermon: 'For myself I should be contented to hear that Sermons were merely unmeaning and harmless . . . as they are, in the instance of the (so-called) Orthodox School. I should be contented if the (so-called) Evangelical Sermons were no worse—but they seem to me in a great many cases hurtful.'[7] Newman goes on to say that there is much that is right in Evangelicalism, and that Evangelicals have the merit of bringing out the Incarnation. But then he continues:

> Yet what I shrink from is their rudeness, irreverence, and almost profaneness; the profaneness of making a most sacred doctrine a subject of vehement declaration, or instrument of exciting the feelings, or topic for vague, general reiterated statement in technical language. Surely this feeling of mine need not arise from the mere fastidiousness of education—it ought to exist in everyone. The poorest and humblest ought to shrink from the lightness and hardness with which a certain school speaks of the adorable works and sufferings of our Saviour. Zaccheus, unrefined as he was, did not intrude himself on our Lord—the woman that was a sinner silently bedewed His feet.[8]

It is the mode of preaching these truths which is at fault, and the question arises, what other way is to be found? Newman finds his answer in the practice of Bishop Butler:

> The peculiarity of Butler is this—that, while on the one hand he is reserved, austere, infrequent in his mention of Christian doctrine, in his writings, yet on the other hand he was very earnest for what he calls in a Charge External Religion, put up a Cross in his private Chapel, and was

[7] Cambridge University Library, Newman to Stephen, 16 March 1835, Add. 7349/15(c) 138.
[8] Ibid.

charged with Popery. I conceive his wonderfully gifted intellect caught the idea which had actually been the rule of the Primitive Church, of teaching the more sacred truths by rites and ceremonies. No mode of teaching can be imagined so public, constant, impressive, permanent, and at the same time reverential than that which makes the doctrine the memorial and declaration of doctrine—reverential, because the very posture of the mind in worship is necessarily such. In this way Christians receive the Gospel literally on their knees, and in a temper altogether different from that critical and argumentative spirit which sitting and listening engender.[9]

Thus Newman wished to bring forward the Services and Catechizing back to their rightful places, which had been usurped by Preaching. Where a doctrine had been delivered over the pulpit in words which were but a feeble representation of the reality, in future Newman wanted the congregation to find the real thing in the Sacraments. Newman expressed this feeling to Wilberforce, in a letter dated a few days before his letter to Stephen:

Again wherever the Holy Eucharist is mentioned there *the Spirit* is mentioned. This is what I meant, which you have not fully apprehended, when I spoke of the Sacraments being the means of persuasion. They are the embodied forms of the Spirit of Christ. And our fault at this day is, that the very *name* of them does not kindle us.[10]

Church services, and the influence of the Holy Spirit will induce the right states of mind, silently as the dew falls, in the mind of the worshipper. And the gain will not only be that notions are exchanged for reality, and that the central citadel of the mind is almost imperceptibly won, but that sacred things and doctrines are no longer exposed to incomprehension and affront.[11] Newman brings out all these ideas to an unknown

[9] Ibid.

[10] Wilberforce Papers, C5, Newman to Wilberforce, 10 March 1835, p. 29.

[11] Cf. *Parochial and Plain Sermons*, London, 1868, vi. 90: first preached 19 April 1841: '. . . the sacred doctrine of the Atoning Sacrifice is not one to be talked of but to be lived upon; not to be put forth irreverently, but to be adored secretly; not to be used as a necessary instrument in the conversion of the ungodly, or for the satisfaction of reasoners of this world, but to be unfolded to the docile and

correspondent in 1843, this time qualifying them slightly. It is plain that now he has the outline firmly established, he has time to work out the finer details:

> I do not object to bringing forward the Atonement explicitly and prominently *in itself*, but under circumstances, i.e. when people are *unfit* to receive it. I think it should be taught all baptized children—that it is the life of all true Christians—but that it is not the *means of conversion* (ordinarily speaking or in the divine appointment) of those who are *not* religious. I think it ought not to be preached to infidels, immoral men, backsliders, at first, but be *reserved* till they begin to feel the need of it. Consequently I object to the use of it so often made in our pulpits as *the one* doctrine to be addressed to *all*. It is but one *out* of others, and not adapted to all.[12]

Newman goes on to say that he would withhold the Incarnation as well as the Atonement, and that he merely wishes to follow the practice of the Apostles and of Christ Himself.

Thus the principle of reserve contributed a good deal to the formation of Newman's ideas on how sacred things were to be handled and communicated. And not for the first time, we notice how reserve is found at close quarters with the other ideas which are so characteristic of Newman—the distinction between real and notional, and the exhortation to act, to put ideas into practice.

During the time of the Oxford Movement, reserve was accorded a role similar to the one it had played in the early Church. That is to say that means had to be found for

---

obedient; to young children, whom the world has not corrupted; to the sorrowful, who need comfort; to the sincere and earnest, who need a rule of life; to the innocent, who need warning; and to the established, who have earned the knowledge of it.'

[12] *Correspondence of John Henry Newman with John Keble and Others, 1839–45.* Ed. at the Birmingham Oratory, London, 1917, p. 205. Cf. *P.S.* i. 307: 8 May 1831: 'Never must we solicitously press the truth upon those who do not profit by what they already possess. It dishonours Christ, while it does the scorner harm, not good. It is casting pearls before swine. We must wait for all opportunities of being useful to men, but beware of attempting too much at once. We must impart the Scripture doctrines, in measure and season, as they can bear them; not being eager to recount them all, rather, hiding them from the world. Seldom must we engage in controversy or dispute; for it lowers the sacred truths to make them a subject for ordinary debate.'

communicating Catholic truth to those who were favourable to it, and there were many who thought that Newman was unscrupulous in the way he brought people to the truth. Many years later, for example, Kingsley's main charge was that Newman had either been unscrupulous or foolish. This charge was made many times in a variety of ways; Abbott continually indulges in sneers against Newman's 'economies'.[13] Even Lord Acton appears to have been fascinated by the problem of Newman's attitude to Truth, and there exist in Cambridge University Library four card-indexes of his, two devoted to extracts from Newman, and the others to notes of Newman's favourite subjects, in which he quotes Newman's dictum that it is no more than a hyperbole to say that a lie may be the nearest thing to the truth three times, quotes a passage from A. P. Stanley to the effect that indifference to truth is the besetting sin of the clerical profession,[14] and another from Ward to the effect that candour is by no means either universally or distinctively characteristic of the saintly mind. The reasons why Newman's manner made this impression on some people will be considered in a later chapter; here I wish to discuss the practical use which Newman found for the precepts of the Church Fathers, and how his practice was modified when he became a Catholic.

The Tractarians made a start by declaring the doctrine of the Apostolical Succession, and by protesting against the reform of the Liturgy, and hoped to introduce the whole circle of Catholic doctrine gradually. The Movement was thus economical in design, and in the following quotation we catch a glimpse of Newman's mind working along these lines:

> Many men . . . have no notion of a *real Presence*. I think Cosin will be useful in opening their minds, and preparing them for your tract. They will, as if against 'Transubstantiation', often say, 'Who doubts this?' 'What repetition is this?' yet all the while will gain something, e.g. I cannot conceive they will think my expressions in the 'Weekday Lecture' *strange*, whatever they may think of their prudence, after reading Cosin. (Moz. ii. 31)

[13] E. A. Abbott, *The Anglican Career of Cardinal Newman*, London, 1892.
[14] R. E. Prothero, *The Life and Correspondence of A. P. Stanley*, London, 1893, ii. 302.

And although the Tracts were apparently unsystematic and fragmentary, they required the reader, in the name of consistency, to accept further Catholic doctrines as they were subsequently brought forward. Other economical methods were adopted in order to prepare the reader for the truth, such as the publication of the book of poems, the *Lyra Apostolica*. It is quite clear, from the following quotation, that such practices depend directly upon the principle of reserve:

> As to the indirect inculcation of the Apostolical doctrines, we have begun the records of the Church with that view. We are printing extracts from Eusebius, &c, . . . to familiarise the imagination of the reader to an Apostolical state of the Church. It was with the same view that we projected our ballads. I had not forgotten Arius's, but his was the abuse of a lawful expedient. What is the 'Lyra Apostolica' but a ballad? It was undertaken with a view of catching people when unguarded. (Moz. i. 483)

Newman touches upon this prudent economy in his sermon on *Wisdom and Innocence*. The sermon is mainly devoted to explaining how the Church came by its reputation for cunning, and then teaches that it is the Church's duty to be wise:

> Thus the servants of Christ are forbidden to defend themselves by violence; but they are not forbidden other means; direct means are not allowed them, but others are even commanded. For instance, *foresight*; 'beware of men:' *avoidance*, 'when they persecute you in this city, flee ye into another:' *prudence and skill*, as in the text, 'Be ye wise as serpents.'[15]

Thus it is plain that Newman and his colleagues consciously employed the methods of the Primitive Church, and saw themselves as leading men on from one truth to another. Froude expresses this feeling most clearly when he writes from the Barbados that he was undermining people, and poisoning their minds. The Tractarians felt that they were in possession of a secret, into which they were initiating those who were favourable, slowly, so as not to frighten them, at the same time

---

[15] *Sermons bearing on Subjects of the Day*, ed. by W. J. Copeland, London, 1869, p. 296: 19 February 1843.

as they were boldly opposing those who were antipathetic to Apostolical principles.

Assuming, then, that the principle of reserve underlay the grand design of the Oxford Movement, it is of interest to see how far Newman's behaviour was governed by this principle. In a letter written to Froude in 1836, he admitted that he was employing economical methods, and his conscience seems a little troubled in consequence: 'As to my economies in my first tracts, I have much to say about them, were not writing a bore. First, I will willingly alter all revilings; again, all serious charges about which I may have changed my mind.'[16] The reader may be justified in thinking that Newman treats 'revilings' and 'serious charges' rather casually. However, Froude acted as Newman's censor, as may be seen in this passage from the *Apologia*:

> I was not unwilling to play with a man, who asked me impertinent questions. I think I had in my mouth the words of the Wise man, 'Answer a fool according to his folly,' especially if he was prying or spiteful. I was reckless of the gossip which was circulated about me; and, when I might easily have set it right, did not deign to do so. Also I used irony in conversation, when matter-of-fact-men would not see what I meant.
>
> This kind of behaviour was a sort of habit with me. If I have ever trifled with my subject, it was a more serious fault. I never used arguments which I saw clearly to be unsound. The nearest approach which I remember to such conduct, but which I consider was clear of it nevertheless, was in the case of Tract 15. The matter of this tract was furnished to me by a friend, to whom I had applied for assistance, but who did not wish to be mixed up with the publication. He gave it me, that I might throw it into shape, and I took his arguments as they stood. In the chief portion of the Tract I fully agreed; . . . but there were arguments, or some argument, in it which I did not follow; I do not recollect what it was. Froude, I think, was disgusted with the whole Tract, and accused me of *economy* in publishing it . . . I think I defended myself with arguments such as these:

that, as every one knew, the Tracts were written by various persons who agreed together in their doctrine, but not always in the arguments by which it was to be proved; that we must be tolerant of differences of opinion among ourselves; that the author of the Tract had a right to his own opinion, and that the argument in question was ordinarily received; that I did not give my own name or authority, nor was asked for my personal belief, but only acted instrumentally, as one might translate a friend's book into a foreign language.

So far one is suspicious of the deployment of all the apparatus of subtle distinctions; the mode of argument is too close to his sophistical justification for his visit to the Opera during his Mediterranean tour.[17] Next he abandons this position, when he says: 'I account these to be good arguments; nevertheless I feel also that such practices admit of easy abuse and are consequently dangerous; but then, again, I feel also this,— that if all such mistakes were to be severely visited, not many men in public life would be left with a character for honour and honesty.'[18] This laborious array of arguments surely indicates that he was uneasy about his Anglican behaviour, and we are left with the impression that in those years Newman employed a not wholly creditable economy. This impression is confirmed in a letter written many years later: 'I think we quite understand each other in re Preachments versus Hints. But not as regards Rogers' reference to what I used to say to him—which was about *economical half speakings*, a very different matter: and these I have given up since I was a Catholic.'[19] We get an idea of what these economies may have been, first from a complaint of Wilson's that Newman was economizing unnecessarily, 'as if to keep your

---

[17] Cf. Moz. i. 315: '. . . I think I have made up my mind about going to operas, &c. I think it allowable—as far as merely going to *see the place*, &c.—in the same sense in which it is allowable to visit the country at all—e.g. I see no objection to going into a heathen country for the sake of seeing it, and going into a playhouse is nothing more than this. If I may not go into a place because bad men are in it, where *can* I go? If, indeed, I go for the sake of the amusement—which would be the case if I *frequented* it—then it would be a different matter; but I go and see, as I go and see a coffee-house, a billiard room, or a mosque. Nor am I supporting persons in a bad way of life—that is, the actors—for if no one went but strangers . . . they would have a poor living.'

[18] *Apo.* 51 f.

[19] *L. and D.* xx. 385.

hand in', and that he had sent Major B. away with the conviction that he looked on D. as a very fine, noble character.[20] We find another example in Newman's letters:

I saw — for a day last week, and was as grave (yet natural) as a judge the whole time, except for one instant, when, to try —, I suddenly on a pause broke out with a sentence like this, turning round sharp: 'So, —, you wish, it seems, to change the monarchy into a republic?' (this was not it, but like it). — shrunk up as if twenty thousand pins had been thrust into him; his flesh goosified, his mouth puckered up, and he looked the picture of astonishment, awe, suspicion and horror. After this trial I went back to my grave manner, and all was well. (Moz. ii. 239)

Of these two passages, it seems that only the second is the genuine economy, and that in the first Wilson took away a false impression from Newman's manner. The significance of this mistake will be discussed in a later chapter.

In the second extract, one finds the exultation of tone unpleasant. It is unfeeling to manipulate one's face and manner like a puppet. Newman's excuse must be that disaster seemed imminent, and that desperate expedients were necessary. We may get a better idea of the seriousness with which he regarded the state of affairs from such remarks as 'Bad times are coming, and no one can tell whether one may not have to travel as Wesley and Whitfield',[21] or 'there is a possibility of a general crash.'[22] Although he lamented that he had the responsibility for the Movement, and found it 'distressing to have to trust one's own judgment on such important matters',[23] he seems to have been peremptory in guiding it. Thus he writes: 'The adventure with Cotton makes me think I shall offend and hurt men I would fain be straight with. Yet what can one do? Men are made of glass: the sooner we break them and get it over the better.'[24] We may suppose that the sense that he had a mission, the feeling that the time was extraordinary, and 'that exuberant and joyous energy with which I had returned from abroad, and which I never had before or since',[25] combined to harden him, and to induce

---

[20] Moz. ii. 207. [21] Moz. i. 391. [22] Moz. ii. 186.
[23] Moz. ii. 46. [24] Moz. i. 458. [25] Apo. 49.

him to behave in this way; his economies of this period are
one with his fierceness of speech and action, either in his tracts,
or in his behaviour to his brother Frank, to whom he addressed
this syllogism: 'I said, "St. Paul bids us avoid those who cause
divisions; you cause divisions: therefore I must avoid you.'[26]
Drastic action was necessary, and he was ready to employ
all means which the Primitive Church had sanctioned.

In an earlier quotation, it was seen that, according to his
own testimony, Newman gave up 'economical half speakings'
when he became a Catholic. It is of some interest to observe
how his behaviour changes as the pressures upon him alter.
The inquiry takes its starting-point from the Appendix to the
Apologia, where Newman tells us that the principle of the
economy is familiarly acted upon every day, and that 'when
we would persuade others, we do not begin by treading on
their toes.' Then he makes this most interesting statement:

> As to the Catholic Religion in England at the present
> day, this only will I observe,—that the truest expedience is
> to answer right out, when you are asked; that the wisest
> economy is to have no management; that the best prudence
> is not to be a coward; that the most damaging folly is to be
> found out shuffling; and that the first of virtues is to 'tell
> truth, and shame the devil'. (*Apo.* 301)

Implicit in this passage is a marked difference between his
practice as an Anglican and as a Catholic. When he was an
Anglican, he was at the head of a Movement, the success of
which imperatively demanded the use of all allowable methods,
but when he became a Catholic, the necessity for this application of the principle of reserve came to an end. And, as to what
he says of the 'truest expedience', it is noteworthy that, as a
Catholic, whenever he has something to say, he says it, and
lets the rest of the world catch up with him, if they are
not ready for it. The best possible example of this is his
behaviour during the 'Consulting the Faithful' turmoil.
Newman had the clearest view that what he was going to say
would be unwelcome to the Bishops, if not before he published
the first part, at least before he published the second part.

[26] *Apo.* 53.

Yet he pressed ahead to finish it, and so it is of great interest
to learn his own opinion of his behaviour at the time:

> I did all I could to ascertain God's will, and that being the
> case, I am sure good will come of my taking it—I am
> of opinion that the Bishops see only one side of things, and
> I have a mission, as far as my own internal feelings go,
> against evils which I see. On the other hand, I have always
> preached that things which are *really* useful, still are done,
> according to God's will, at one time, not at another—and
> that, if you attempt at a wrong time, what in itself is right,
> you perhaps become a heretic or schismatic. What I may
> aim at may be real and good, but it may be God's will it
> should be done a hundred years later. . . . When I am gone,
> it will be seen perhaps that persons stopped me from doing a
> work which I might have done. God overrules all things. Of
> course it is discouraging to be out of joint with the time, and
> to be snubbed and stopped as soon as I begin to act. (*L.
> and D.* xix. 179)

We see here that Newman acted upon a call, although he knew
that such action was bound to be unpopular. Secondly, he
speaks of 'my own internal feelings', and 'evils which I see',
which surely suggests that he is setting his own opinion against
the opinions of others. Next, he thinks that he chose to speak
at an unwise time, which means in effect that he should have
reserved his speech. So far we are left with the impression that
Newman regretted that he had spoken out, and felt that he
should have employed the economical methods of his Anglican
days, but when he makes the hypothesis that a later age would
see that he had been stopped in a necessary work, we see that
he thinks he was right to speak out, and that economy was
unnecessary.

Of course, that Newman chose to speak out, eschewing reserve, marks his changing attitude to ecclesiastical authority,
but it also emphasizes the important point that he is no
longer a party-man. He no longer has to consider the interests
of a small but growing party, and hence no longer has to guard
his speech to gain immediate objectives. This feeling that he
is his own man can be detected at an early stage in his

Catholic career, in the letters he published in Henry Wilberforce's *Weekly Register*; there he tells us:

> One of the main secrets of success is self-reliance. This seems
> a strange sentiment for a Christian journalist to utter, but
> we speak of self in contrast, not with a higher power, but
> with our fellow-men. He who leans on others, instead of
> confiding in his own right arm, will do nothing great. Here,
> again, we must explain; for is this not the sentiment of
> every wild religionist who makes himself his own prophet
> and guide, and despises Holy Fathers and ecclesiastical
> rulers? Well, then, we are censuring dependence on others,
> when others are not representatives, in so far as they are
> relied on, of a higher and more sacred authority. We hope
> we have expressed ourselves without any paradox at last.
> (*L. and D*. xviii. 580)

The passage is uncharacteristic of Newman, because it does not
argue steadily and inexorably forward, but seems instead to
feel its way round difficulties as they arise. The reason for this
is that Newman is establishing a new concept, of self-reliance
which, without plunging into the error of private judgement,
is outside the sphere of ecclesiastical authority.[27] As an
Anglican, he had been committed to a party, and this had
demanded the use of reserve for prudential reasons, but as a
Catholic he was committed to nothing but the prosperity of the
Church. He could speak out if he wished, and so needed a
theory of self-reliance upon which to found what he said.
Ward publishes a letter of Newman's, in which he expresses
this new feeling, only possible in a changed state of affairs,
that there was a danger of being too reserved:

> I know well that 'all things have their season,' and
> that there is not only 'a time to keep silence,' but 'a time
> to speak,' and that, in some states of society, such as our
> own, it is the worst charity, and the most provoking, irritat-
> ing rule of action, and the most unhappy policy, not to
> speak out, not to suffer to be spoken out, all that there is to

---

[27] Cf. *L. and D*. xxi. 331: 'Nothing great or living can be done except when men
are self governed and independent: this is quite consistent with a full maintenance
of ecclesiastical supremacy.'

say. Such speaking out is under such circumstances the triumph of religion, whereas concealment, accommodation, and evasion is to co-operate with the spirit of error,—but it is not always so.[28]

It is therefore clear that Newman no longer believed that one should employ economy for politic reasons, either because he found that it was no longer necessary, or because the cautious communication of knowledge was not as effective as to tell the truth straight out. But there still remained a place for the principle of reserve; we note that he says 'it is not always so', and that sometimes it is necessary to conceal and evade. When he became a Catholic, reserve manifested itself as a censor of extravagance, instead of as a deliberate policy of leading the Protestant mind on to Catholic truth by means of carefully measured gradations. Thus, speaking of the excesses of devotion such as Faber's, Newman says: 'And, as spoken by man to man, in England, in the nineteenth century, I consider them calculated to prejudice inquirers, to frighten the unlearned, to unsettle consciences, to provoke blasphemy, and to work the loss of souls.'[29] Similarly he urged Simpson and Acton, the proprietors of the *Rambler*, to avoid theology and other dangerous topics such as the Temporal Power of the Pope, and thought that Simpson had no reason to complain of the treatment he received, asking 'Why did he begin? why did he fling about ill sounding words on sacred and delicate subjects?'[30] And in his *Letter to the Duke of Norfolk*, Newman accused the newspapers of showing insufficient restraint; he felt deeply the violence and cruelty of journals and other publications, 'which, taking as they professed to do the Catholic side, employed themselves by their rash language . . . in unsettling the weak in faith, throwing back inquirers, and shocking the Protestant mind'.[31] The principle of reserve continues to counsel prudence and caution, just as it had done in the Primitive Church, and ensures that teachers are careful how they dispense knowledge, and do not frighten those whom they might have converted had they been more discriminating in their use of language. Newman held

[28] Wilfrid Ward, *The Life of John Henry Cardinal Newman*, London, 1912, ii. 424.
[29] *Certain Difficulties felt by Anglicans in Catholic Teaching*, London, 1876, ii. 115.
[30] *L. and D.* xx. 391.   [31] *Diff.* ii. 300.

that the main task confronting Catholics was to disabuse
Protestants of the prejudice they felt against Catholic doctrines; at the time he was preparing the Lectures published as
the *Present Position of Catholics*, he wrote that 'our line is, not to
attack the Church of England, which is low game, but to remove prejudices against ourselves . . .'[32] Thus there was no
need to repeat his practice as an Anglican, and to inculcate
doctrines by reserving them, but there was a lot to be gained by
repressing excesses such as those of Faber and Ward; the emphasis of reserve changed from leading people on to ensuring
that they should not find unnecessary obstacles in their way.

In addition to this change of emphasis, we note a difference
in Newman's attitude to devotion when he became a Catholic.
The principle of reserve fostered reverential behaviour
towards sacred things by withholding them, so that one should
not become familiar with them. It was in this spirit that Newman was 'much offended at the very irreverent exhibitions of
the Crucifix, and of the souls in purgatory . . . which are stuck
about as puffs are on the London walls',[33] when he was in
Rome during his Mediterranean trip. Similarly, it was one
of his main points against the Romanists in the *Prophetical
Office of the Church* that they trod incautiously on holy ground,
and arranged, explained, exhausted every part of the Divine
economy. He felt that the neatness and finish which they sought
was 'destructive of many of the most noble and most salutary
exercises of mind in the individual Christian', and went on:

> That feeling of awe which the mysteriousness of the Gospel
> should excite, fades away under this fictitious illumination
> which is poured over the entire Dispensation . . . what
> amount of temporal punishment must be set against the
> sins of accepted Christians? what sort of change takes
> place in the Eucharist? . . . these are questions which man
> cannot determine, yet such as the Romanists delight to
> handle. Not content with what is revealed, they are ever
> intruding into things not seen as yet, and growing
> familiar with mysteries; gazing upon the ark of God
> over boldly and long, till they venture to put out the
> hand and touch it.[34]

[32] *L. and D.* xiv. 214.   [33] Moz. i. 392.
[34] *The Via Media of the Anglican Church*, London, 1877, i. 91 f.

And he felt that the great glory of the Church of England was that it was reverent; in the *University Sermons* he wrote:

> Far different [i.e. from the Roman Church] is the spirit of our own Church, which, rejoicing, as she does, to find her children walking in truth, never forgets the dignity and preciousness of the gifts she offers; as appears, for instance, in the warnings prefacing the Communion Service, and in the Commination,—above all, in the Athanasian Creed, in which she but follows the example of the early Church, which first withdrew her mysteries from the many, then, when controversy exposed them, guarded them with an anathema,—in each case, lest curious Reason might rashly gaze and perish. (*U.S.* 71: 11 December 1831)

While Newman remained to the end of his life scrupulous about sacred things—ever more scrupulous, when he had to handle relics or altar stones—we can detect a change in his attitude to the nature of reverence itself. He is still 'frightened at the chance of being satirical etc before the Blessed Sacrament',[35] when he has to lecture in church, but now we find him accepting a situation where reverence can become a habit of mind without being the less reverent for being a habit. Thus he expresses his opinion that Protestants are not certain of their doctrines, and feel they ought to believe them, and try to believe them:

> They feel very clear and quite satisfied, while they are very still; but if they turn about their head, or change their posture ever so little, the vision of the Unseen, like a mirage, is gone from them. So they keep the exhibition of their faith for high days and great occasions, when it comes forth with sufficient pomp and gravity of language, and ceremonial of manner. . . . They condemn Catholics, because, however religious they may be, they are natural, unaffected, easy, and cheerful, in their mention of sacred things; and they think themselves never so real as when they are especially solemn. (*Diff.* i. 254)

There is a fundamental change here. The difference seems to be that when he was an Anglican, he tried to screw up a

[35] *L. and D.* xiii. 468.

people who had become dead to real religious feeling to an unaccustomed pitch of reverence. This he had attempted to do by going back to the pattern of antiquity, by withholding sacred things, and so could never have approved of the word 'easy' in the last quotation. But when he became a Catholic, he found that Catholics had a different habit of mind from Anglicans and Protestants, one in which reverence for sacred things was second nature. In other words, he was attaching new meaning to the word 'faith', which he explained in the same volume; Protestants considered that faith and love were the same, and did not 'think the inconsistency possible of really believing without obeying'. But Catholics held that

> faith and love, faith and obedience, faith and works, are simply separable, and ordinarily separated, in fact; that faith does not imply love, obedience, or works; that the firmest faith, so as to move mountains, may exist without love,—that is, real faith, as really faith in the strict sense of the word as the faith of a martyr or a doctor. In other words, when Catholics speak of faith, they are contemplating the existence of a gift which Protestantism does not even imagine. Faith is a spiritual sight of the unseen; and since in matter of fact Protestantism does not impart this sight, does not see the unseen, has no experience of this habit, this act of the mind—therefore, since it retains the word 'faith', it is obliged to find some other meaning for it. (*Diff*. i. 236)

He found that Catholics already possessed the reverence for sacred things which at Oxford he had tried to inculcate by means of the principle of reserve. Catholics did not need to be 'screwed up' to a greater pitch of reverence; they could be trusted to remain reverent even while they were 'easy', and so this particular application of the principle of reserve lost its usefulness.

Together with this disuse of the formal application of the principle, we find a disposition to trust the laity, and to rely upon them to a greater extent. At the time of publishing the *Arians*, Newman had no belief in the ability of the untrained mind to avoid perplexing itself in theological affairs; he felt that such matters should be reserved for those who were able to understand them. He said, for example, that

> The error of the ancient Sophists had consisted in their indulging without restraint or discrimination in the discussion of practical topics, whether religious or political, instead of selecting such as might exercise, without demoralizing, their minds. The rhetoricians of Christian times introduced the same error into their treatment of the highest and most sacred subjects of theology. (*Ari.* 32)

The point to notice here is not his strictures against those of more subtle intellect, who led astray their simpler brethren; as we have seen from the cases of Simpson and Acton, these he repeated throughout his life. Of more importance is the assumption that the simpler brethren *will* be led astray. He assumes much the same sort of thing in the *University Sermons* when he says:

> Our great danger is . . . lest we rashly take the Scriptures from the Church's custody, and commit them to the world, that is, to what is called public opinion; which men boast, indeed, will be right on the whole, but which, in fact, being the opinion of men who, as a body, have not cultivated the internal moral sense, and have externally no immutable rules to bind them, is, in religious questions, only by accident right, or only on very broad questions, and tomorrow will betray interests which today it affects to uphold. (*U.S.* 73: 11 December 1831)

What one really misses here are the words 'the faithful'. Newman does not envisage the possibility of there being a body of men who are *not* deceived by sophistical reasonings, and who *have* a moral sense sufficiently developed for them to be accepted by the Church as worthy defenders of the faith. Putting this another way, one doubts whether, if at this time an Anglican Ullathorne had asked Newman 'Who are the laity?' Newman would have answered as he did in 1859, 'that the Church would look foolish without them—*not* those words'.[36]

---

[36] *L. and D.* xix. 141.

What I am driving at will be plain by now; if the Catholic system considered that the faithful held implicitly what the Church might later wish to define, so that the Church would be able to consult them, then the laity would assume more importance than under the Anglican system. The Church would preserve the true religion by codifying it, but the laity would have it engraved upon their hearts, and so Newman seems more disposed to trust them not to run astray. This shift indicates a slight inconsistency in his Anglican position, for one of the great conclusions of the *Arians of the Fourth Century* was that during the Arian controversy it was the clergy who had been deceived by the heresy, while the laity had remained faithful. The reason for this inconsistency seems to be that his view of the clergy in their teaching aspect obscured his view of the laity as those who maintained the faith. And since he grew to trust the laity, and to form his opinion that 'they may be made in this day the strength of the Church',[37] he no longer needed to employ reserve towards them, and so we find that he prefers to be more generous:

> Life has the same right to decay, as it has to wax strong. This is especially the case with great ideas. You may stifle them; or you may refuse them elbow-room; or again, you may torment them with your continual meddling; or you may let them have free course and range, and be content, instead of anticipating their excesses, to expose and restrain those excesses after they have occurred. But you have only this alternative; and for myself, I prefer much wherever it is possible, to be first generous and then just; to grant full liberty of thought, and to call it to account when abused. (*Diff.* ii. 79)

Where he had employed the principle of reserve to exercise an anxious restraint over ideas, he now awaits the providential outcome of things. To put this another way, the Catholic Newman had greater faith in the future, and more confidence that all would be well, than the Anglican Newman. This is a natural consequence of belonging to a large, 'Catholic', community, rather than to a small party which had to struggle

[37] *L. and D.* xiv. 252.

to maintain its claim of catholicity.[38] In the *Present Position of Catholics*, he outlines what he wants of the laity:

> I want a laity, not arrogant, not rash in speech, not disputatious, but men who know their religion, who enter into it, who know just where they stand, who know what they hold, and what they do not, who know their creed so well, that they can give an account of it, who know so much of history that they can defend it. I want an intelligent, well-instructed laity; I am not denying you are such already: but I mean to be severe, and, as some would say, exorbitant in my demands. I wish you to enlarge your knowledge, to cultivate your reason, to get an insight into the relation of truth to truth, to learn to view things as they are, to understand how faith and reason stand to each other, what are the bases and principles of Catholicism, and where lie the main inconsistencies and absurdities of the Protestant theory. I have no apprehension you will be the worse Catholics for familiarity with these subjects, provided you cherish a vivid sense of God above, and keep in mind that you have souls to be judged and saved. . . .[39]

His judgement of what may reasonably be expected of the laity has advanced a good deal from the time when, speaking of Knox and Coleridge, he said 'both these men are laymen, and that is remarkable. The very stones cry out.'[40] Moreover, it is interesting to note how he answers the objection that his Anglican self would have urged, that sacred things should be withheld lest men should become familiar with them; familiarity with such subjects will not be dangerous, unless the inquirer becomes forgetful of God, and pursues them for their own sake. It is amusing to speculate that this new and 'liberal' Newman may have come into existence as a result of

---

[38] This line of argument is best illustrated by a conversation between J. W. Knott and Newman, related to Isaac Williams: 'he [Newman] said that he now saw that his teaching while with us had a Semi-Pelagian tendency, that he did not then clearly distinguish between nature and grace; that he would now set forth the Atonement as an instrument of conversion, whereas he would have kept it back while with us.' Letters and papers in the possession of Dr. Emily Williams, 6 October 1854, quoted by O. W. Jones, *Isaac Williams and his Circle*, London, 1971, p. 131.
[39] *Lectures on the Present Position of Catholics in England*, London, 1880, p. 390.
[40] Moz. ii. 93.

his experience of the reserve practised towards him by Catholic
churchmen; for example, he protests that 'English Catholics
are not so scandalizable as some good men in Rome think—
they seem to me to look at us as half converted, and they
dandle us like babies, speaking under correction. They try
to manage us, when open speaking is best. We can bear "strong
meat".'[41] The use of the phrase 'strong meat' plainly casts
an eye towards the old Tractarian practice; the contrast
between his old position and his new is therefore made explicit.
It is interesting to note, besides, that he uses the same sort of
language to describe the theologians of the time:

> Our theological philosophers are like the old nurses who
> wrap the unhappy infant in swaddling bands or boards—
> put a lot of blankets over him—and shut the windows that
> not a breath of fresh air may come to his skin—as if he
> were not healthy enough to bear wind and water in due
> measures. They move in a groove, and will not tolerate
> any one who does not move in the same. (*L. and D.* xxiv. 316)

At much the same time, he told Pusey to bring forward his
strong points, saying that he had no sympathy for the policy
of suppression: 'I have no fear that it will harm the cause of
what I think truth, that some things, nay strong things can be
adduced against it. There are objections, and grave objections,
to the simplest truths, and the cause of Truth gains by their
being stated clearly and considered carefully.'[42]

It has been seen that Newman started by wishing to lead
people on by means of the principle of reserve, and that he
ended by believing that the best and most manly course was to
speak out, whatever the consequences. This change reflects
the move from Tractarianism to Catholicism; he no longer
had to induce people to accept Catholic doctrines, and so had
no need to employ reserve; instead, reserve was used to censor
excesses on the Catholic side. But it also reflects a change in
his character; one feels that sometimes, as an Anglican, he
enjoyed pulling the strings, and watching his puppets dance.
When he became a Catholic, he seems to have lost some of this
desire; it is possible to say, in contrast to Coleridge during the
Achilli trial, that Catholicism improved his character.

[41] *L. and D.* xix. 332.   [42] *L. and D.* xxiii. 284.

So far, the applications of the principle of reserve which have been considered have had an influence on methods and practice only. It is now time to trace the principle of reserve in the doctrines which Newman taught in the pulpit.

CHAPTER THREE

THE PROVIDENTIAL WORKINGS
OF GOD

IN the first chapter it was seen that the principle of reserve is closely connected with a particular understanding of what is expressed by the word 'God'. Since He is a God who is infinite, incomprehensible to our limited capacity, He is a God who hides Himself from us. And the idea that God is hidden was familiar to Newman from a very early age. In the *Apologia* he records that, as a schoolboy, he thought he might be an angel, and that his fellow angels by a playful device were concealing themselves from him, and deceiving him with the semblance of a material world.[1] The reader constantly comes across the same idea in the *Autobiographical Writings*; in spring 1817 Newman wrote a sermon on the text, 'Great things doeth He, which we cannot comprehend',[2] and on 2 February 1823 he made a note about the way in which the Bible glories in mystery, and how it 'seems to delight in setting the two doctrines [i.e. that God is sole worker, while man is co-operator] in direct opposition to each other'.[3] And among the sermons preached at St. Clement's in 1825 is a group of three preached on the text, 'Verily, Thou art a God that hidest Thyself', in which he argued that God must be sought 'in *a certain* way and in *a certain frame* of mind',[4] otherwise He will remain hidden. In the second sermon he teaches that God hides Himself from 'the sincere but weakhearted and feeble Christian . . . in mercy that the inquirer may seek the more earnestly— Had we spiritual blessings granted us immediately we asked for them, we should learn to think little of them—That which is obtained easily, is regarded cheaply.'[5] Ignorance, he asserts, 'actually has a tendency to *improve* the soul'.[6]

---

[1] *Apo.* 16.   [2] *A.W.* 154.   [3] *A.W.* 170.
[4] Newman Archives, Birmingham Oratory, unpublished sermon no. 47, p. 8.
[5] Unpublished sermon no. 48, p. 1.
[6] Ibid., p. 10.

Newman employs the principle of reserve widely in his volumes of sermons to account for a variety of different problems. Since Divine matters are incomprehensible to the human mind, the historical revelation must necessarily have been incomplete, and so difficulties came into existence, which might be stumbling-blocks to faith. It was Newman's pastoral duty to elucidate these difficulties, and he drew heavily on the principle of reserve to account for them. The fundamental position that there *are* difficulties as a result of the incomplete communication of religious knowledge is brought out in the sermon on the *Christian Mysteries:*

> By meditation we detect in Revelation this remarkable principle, which is not openly propounded, *that religious light is intellectual darkness.* As if our gracious Lord had said to us: 'Scripture does not *aim* at making mysteries, but they are as shadows brought out by the Sun of Truth. When you knew nothing of revealed light, you knew not revealed darkness. Religious truth requires you should be told *something*, your own imperfect nature prevents your knowing *all*; and to know *something*, and *not all*,—*partial knowledge*,—must of course perplex; doctrines imperfectly revealed must be mysterious.'
> Such being the necessary mysteriousness of Scripture doctrine, how can we best turn it to account in the contest which we are engaged in with our evil hearts? Now we are given to see how to do this in part, and, as far as we see, let us be thankful for the gift. It seems, then, that difficulties in revelation are especially given to prove the *reality of our faith.* (*P.S.* i. 211: 14 June 1829)

We note here the characteristic way in which Newman boldly converts a difficulty into a point in his favour. Moreover, we see how Newman guides his argument so that he passes easily from the difficulties created by the partial communication of knowledge to the distinction which is of such great importance in Newman's writings, the distinction between real assent to a doctrine, so that it becomes entirely assimilated into the mind, and notional assent, when one professes to believe in a doctrine, without actually acting upon that belief. The sheer harmony of the arrangement as Newman explains it shows that it must be divinely appointed; it is like a jigsaw which has only one solution, for the beauty of the method and the economical use of materials are in themselves a powerful argument that this is the correct solution.

Reserve in God's dealings with us is not only necessary because of our finite faculties, but because it is His customary method to employ partial representations towards us. In this way, Newman draws typology within the orbit of reserve:

> And thus, too, all that is bright and beautiful, even on the surface of this world, though it has no substance, and may not suitably be enjoyed for its own sake, yet is a figure and promise of that true joy which issues out of the Atonement. It is a promise beforehand of what is to be: it is a shadow, raising hope because the substance is to follow, but not to be rashly taken instead of the substance. And it is God's usual mode of dealing with us, in mercy to send the shadow before the substance, that we may take comfort in what is to be, before it comes. Thus our Lord before His Passion rode into Jerusalem in triumph, with the multitudes crying Hosanna, and strewing His road with palm branches and their garments. (*P.S.* vi. 92: 9 April 1841)[7]

In accordance with this practice, 'most of the great appointments of Divine goodness are marked by this very character of what men call *exclusiveness*. God distributes numberless benefits to all men, but He does so through a few select instruments.'[8] Just as God sends the shadow before the substance, He dispenses religious knowledge first to a chosen few. Newman interpreted Jesus' conduct by means of this idea, and found, first, that Jesus employed the same methods.

[7] Cf. *P.S.* ii. 85: 23 November 1834: '[Prophecies] . . . are merely instances of the harmonious movement of God's word and deed, His sealing up events from the first, His introducing them once and for all, though they are but gradually unfolded to our limited faculties, and in this transitory scene.' Cf. also *P.S.* v. 100: 11 February 1838: '[God's] dispensations move forward in an equable uniform way, like circles expanding about one centre; the greater good to come being, not indeed the same as the past good, but nevertheless resembling it, as a substance resembles its type.'

[8] *P.S.* iii. 194: 29 November 1829. Cf. *S.D.* 193: 13 November 1842: 'And let it be observed, that the sacred writers show themselves quite aware of this peculiarity in the mode in which God's purposes are carried on from age to age. They are frequent in speaking of a "remnant" as alone inheriting the promises; the phenomenon of a remnant has been a sort of law of the Divine Dispensations . . .'

Now, on the other hand, let us contemplate the means which His Divine Wisdom actually adopted with a view of making His resurrection subservient to the propagation of His Gospel.—He showed Himself openly, not to all the people, but unto witnesses chosen before of God. It is, indeed, a *general* characteristic of the course of His providence to make the few the channels of His blessings to the many; but in the instance we are contemplating, a few were selected, because only a few *could* (humanly speaking) be made instruments. (*P.S.* i. 286: 24 April 1831)

The Apostles had to be certain that it was Jesus Himself who had risen, and the 'thought of Him was to be stamped upon their minds as the one master-spring of their whole course of life for the future.'[9] By following this line of argument Newman is able to show that there would have been no point in Jesus' showing Himself to the whole Jewish people after the Resurrection, and that this procedure would have defeated the 'real object of His rising again, the propagation of His Gospel through the world by *means of His own intimate friends* and followers'.[10]

Not only was knowledge withheld from the world, and only dispensed through selected instruments, but reserve was practised towards those very instruments:

Our Lord had secret meanings when He spoke, and did not bring forth openly all His divine sense at once. He knew what He was about to do from the first, but He wished to lead forward His disciples, and to arrest and open their minds, before He instructed them: for all cannot receive His words, and on the blind and deaf the most sacred truths fall without profit.

And thus, throughout the course of His gracious dispensations from the beginning, it may be said that the Author and Finisher of our faith has hid things from us in mercy, and listened to our questionings, while He Himself knew what He was about to do. He has hid, in order afterwards to reveal, that then, on looking back on what He said and did before, we may see in it what at the

9 *P.S.* i. 286.   10 *P.S.* i. 290.

time we did not see, and thereby see it to more profit. (*P.S.* vii. 160: 20 May 1838)

There are two important points to notice here. The first is that the completion of the revelation reopens, as it were, a case which had been closed. The facts of history had passed, bearing upon their face their own interpretation, and then more facts were disclosed, which threw fresh light upon the earlier revelation. The process ensured that the later and proper interpretation was kept fresh and undulled. To take an example of this, as far as the Tractarians were concerned, the Anglican formularies had preserved, almost by accident, a mass of Catholic truth. They were thought to bear an entirely Protestant interpretation, and so had been suffered to survive, familiar and apparently well known. Yet when Catholic truths were being recovered for the Church of England, it was seen that the formularies had in fact been the repository of these Catholic truths, and had kept them the more pristine for being concealed. And so the hand of Providence was to be seen in the way Catholic doctrines were recovered from the supposedly Protestant formularies. It is no wonder that the Tractarians were elated, when it was given to them to perceive what had lain hidden and reserved for so many years. Thus this process of reinterpretation enables men to see behind the veil—to note the course of God's Providence, and to gain an insight into what otherwise remains hidden.

Secondly, we see how a merciful means of communicating knowledge is adopted; it is dispensed gradually, and so we find Newman arguing that 'Christ's commandments, viewed *as He enjoins them on us*, are not grievous. They *would* be grievous if put upon us all at once; but they are *not* heaped on us, according to *His* order of dispensing them, which goes upon an harmonious and considerate plan; by little and little, first one duty, then another, then both, and so on.'[11] The spectacle of revelation being adjusted on our behalf would undoubtedly impress many who would otherwise find themselves baffled by the impossibility of predicating anything of Providence.

Christ not only hid things from us; He hid Himself: 'Our Saviour said most plainly, that He was the Son of God; but it is

[11] *P.S.* i. 104: 5 June 1831.

one thing to declare the whole truth, another to receive it. Our
Saviour said all that need be said, but His Apostles understood Him not.'[12] Newman argues that the Apostles and
disciples did not understand what Jesus said, and concludes:

> And when we look into our Saviour's conduct in the days
> of His flesh, we find that He purposely concealed that
> knowledge, which yet He gave; as if intending it should
> be enjoyed, but not at once; as if His words were to stand,
> but to wait awhile for their interpretation; as if reserving
> them for His coming, who at once was to bring Christ and
> His words into the light. (*P.S.* iv. 255: 7 May 1837)

Just as Christ is merciful in the way He discloses His commandments, He is merciful in the way He reveals Himself, and we
should model our own methods of preaching on His. Those
who are agitated and restless are made more restless and
unhappy by holding out to them doctrines and assurances
which they cannot rightly apprehend. But if people just set
themselves to obey God, 'we learn to view Him in His tranquil
providence, before we set about contemplating His greater
works. . . . Thus our Saviour gradually discloses Himself to the
troubled mind; not as He is in heaven, as when He struck
down Saul to the ground, but as He was in the days of His
flesh, eating and conversing among His brethren.'[13] And so
Christ hides Himself, the better to disclose Himself: but He
also hides Himself lest we be overcome by His presence:

> The truth is, we Christians know too much concerning
> Him to endure the open manifestation of His greatness.
> It is in mercy that He hides Himself from those who would
> be overcome by the sensible touch of the Almighty Hand.
> Still it is plain that, after all, in spite of this considerate
> regard for our frailness, His visitation cannot but be awful
> anyhow, to creatures who know what we know, and are
> what we are. This cannot be avoided; the very secrecy of
> His coming has its solemnity: is it not fearful to wait for Him,
> appalling to receive Him, a burden to have held communion
> with Him? (*S.D.* 139: 22 May 1831)[14]

---

[12] *P.S.* iv. 254: 7 May 1837.   [13] *P.S.* i. 241: 14 November 1830.

[14] Cf. *S.D.* 44: 30 October 1842: 'Moreover, even if we could possibly have the
views of God and of ourselves, which are the simple truth, it would not be good for
us to have them,—they would be too much for us.'

And because He is hidden, our responsibility is great; we have to discern His presence, and to approach Him reverently:

> Next, if He is still on earth, yet is not visible (which cannot be denied), it is plain that He keeps Himself still in the condition which He chose in the days of His flesh. I mean, He is a hidden Saviour, and may be approached (unless we are careful) without due reverence and fear. (*P.S.* iv. 249: 25 December 1837)

But although Christ's hiddenness adds to our responsibility, it is also a means of drawing us on; it teaches us proper reverence. Christ disclosed Himself to few, because 'fear must go before love. Till he who has authority shows he has it and can use it, his forbearance will not be valued duly; his kindness will look like weakness. We learn to contemn what we do not fear; and we cannot love what we contemn. So in religion also. We cannot understand Christ's mercies till we understand His power, His glory, His unspeakable holiness, and our demerits; that is, until we first fear Him.'[15]

Thus by emphasizing the need for reverential fear, Newman recovers an unpopular side of religion, and provides a solid basis for Tractarian asceticism. The close connection between fear and asceticism can be plainly seen in this quotation: 'This is to feed ourselves *with* fear. Thus let us proceed in the use of all our privileges, and all will be benefits. Let us not keep festivals without keeping vigils; let us not keep Eastertide without observing Lent.'[16] Fear must be a fundamental part of religion, if Christ hides Himself, and so Newman is able to assert what he says time and time again, that religion is a serious business, and which should have an effect upon every man who professes to be religious.

Another great lesson which we learn from Christ's hiddenness is that we are entirely ignorant. 'Take, for instance, His temptation. Why was it undergone at all, seeing our redemption is ascribed to His death, not to it? Why was it so long? What took place during it? . . . These and many other questions admit of no satisfactory solution.'[17] Newman goes on to say:

[15] *P.S.* i. 304: 8 May 1831.   [16] *S.D.* 122: 1 May 1842.
[17] *P.S.* iii. 158: 8 March 1835.

I bring together these various questions in order to impress upon you our depth of ignorance on the entire subject under review. The Dispensation of mercy is revealed to us in its great and blessed result, our redemption, and in one or two other momentous points. Upon all these we ought to dwell and enlarge, mindfully and thankfully, but with the constant recollection that after all, as regards the Dispensation itself, only one or two partial notices are revealed to us altogether of a great Divine Work. (*P.S.* iii. 159: 8 March 1835)

It will be remarked how devastatingly Newman takes over the sceptic's position, and shows how the inconsistencies and deficiencies in the believer's case merely provide further proof that God generally acts upon the principle of reserve. But more important still, we see how absolutely this demonstration of our ignorance excludes any possibility of arrogance or intellectual pride. When we know how much is reserved from us, all that is possible is simple faith.

Later in life, Newman adopted a variation of this argument in a letter to an unknown correspondent:

Can you know about God's dealings with others, since *He* sees their heart and you do not? but you can know something of His dealings with yourself. Now has He not ever been most loving and tender with you, and have not you been most ungrateful to Him? What you *know* is His dealings with *you*—what you *don't* understand, is His dealings with others. Go by what you know, instead of attempting what you don't know—Interpret what you don't know by what you do. (*L. and D*. xxiii. 260)

At another time, Newman employs this train of thought in an attempt to check the reforming and innovating tendencies of his time; after pointing out that there are many questions which the reason wishes to ask, he asserts that faith wishes for no more than is given, and then goes on to say:

The whole system of what is called cause and effect, is one of mystery; and this instance, if it may be called one, supplies abundant matter of praise and adoration to a pious mind. It suggests to us, equally with the topics which

have already come before us, how very much our knowledge of God's ways is but on the surface. What are those
deep hidden reasons why Christ went and the Spirit came?
Marvellous and glorious, beyond our understanding! Let
us worship in silence; meanwhile, let us jealously maintain
this, and every other portion of our Creed, lest, by dropping
jot or tittle, we suffer the truths concealed therein to escape
from us. (*P.S.* ii. 213: end of 1834)

A train of thought such as this, while rendering controversy
impertinent and ridiculous, might leave him open to charges
of fideism or obscurantism. So, with that balance which is
characteristically his, Newman draws out the consequences
and implications of the doctrine that much knowledge has
been withheld from us. Much has been reserved; therefore,
'let us worship in silence'. But at the same time, a revelation
has been made, which cannot have been made for nothing,
and which should therefore be jealously guarded.

Elsewhere, Newman uses the same argument to assert the
importance of the clergy's responsibility, and the trust reposed
in them. Since we do not know what is the final object of the
Gospel Revelation, we must not pick and choose from the
Gospel, but must transmit it as faithfully as possible:

This consideration is an answer to those who would limit
our message to what is influential and convincing in it, and
measure its divinity by its success. But I have introduced it
rather to show generally, how utterly we are in the dark
about the whole subject; and therefore, as being in the dark,
how necessary it is to gird our garments about us, and hold
fast our treasure, and hasten forward, lest we betray our
trust. We have no means of knowing how far a small mistake
in the Faith may carry us astray. (*P.S.* ii. 268: end of 1834)

And again, it is in a similar manner that Newman expressed
the deep Tractarian consciousness of the pregnancy of each of
Christ's words, perhaps captured most clearly in a letter of
Keble's, in which he recalls a walk during which they had
discussed the idea that each word of Christ's is in itself a Church
Canon. Newman puts the question at its lowest when he says
it is remarkable that there should be difficulties on the face of

Scripture, and goes on to conclude that 'He who speaks is not one whose thoughts it is easy to get possession of; that it is no light matter to put one's-self, even in part, into the position of His mind, and to state under what feelings and motives He said this or that; in a word, I wish to impress upon you, that our Saviour's words are not of a nature to be heard once and no more, but that to understand them we must feed upon them, and live in them, as if by little and little growing into their meaning.'[18] It is we who are at fault; we are unable to comprehend the full meaning, and so Newman wrote:

> Doubtless Christ spoke no words in vain. The Eternal Wisdom of God did not utter His voice that we might at once catch up His words in an irreverent manner, think we understand them at a glance, and pass them over. But His word endureth for ever; it has a depth of meaning suited to all times and places, and hardly and painfully to be understood in any. (*P.S.* i. 28: 2 September 1832)

We are in the presence of the principle which is more than anything fundamental to the *Essay on the Development of Christian Doctrine*; that the human mind cannot retain all the aspects of a great idea at the same time, and that the only way to grasp all the bearings of an idea is to allow the mind to dwell upon it, so that its various aspects can be developed. Ideas, or in this case the words of Christ, withhold their full meaning until we are able and worthy to comprehend them. Thus Newman may have conceived of ideas as informed by the principle of reserve, disclosing their secrets gradually to the earnest seeker of truth.

The various aspects which have so far been drawn out in this chapter may be summarized in one remarkable quotation from the *Parochial Sermons*:

> What is true in these instances, is true of all the parts of our Lord's gracious economy. He was 'manifested in the flesh; justified in the Spirit; seen of Angels; preached unto the Gentiles; believed on in the world; received up into glory;' yet what was the nature of the manifestation? The Annunciation was secret; the Nativity was secret;

[18] *P.S.* iii. 130: 12 April 1835.

the miraculous Fasting in the wilderness was secret; the Resurrection secret; the Ascension not far from secret; the abiding Presence secret. One thing alone was public, and in the eyes of the world,—His Death; the only event which did not speak of His divinity, the only event in which He seemed a sign, not of power, but of weakness. (*P.S.* vi. 113: 12 November 1837)

Much, therefore, has been withheld from us. But it is equally certain that there has been a revelation, and the Church ordinances find their proper weight and position as the link between the two, and so Newman tells us we should consider God's ordinances as 'anticipations and first-fruits of that sight of Him which one day must be'.[19] From the knowledge that reserve is practised towards us, we can arrive at an empirical justification of worship and Church ordinances; they remove the veil between God and us, and prepare us for its total removal. Moreover, worship is assigned its rightful place in the system which is being woven; a new element is drawn within the system, and both sustains it, and is sustained by it, in a way which reminds us of Newman's idea that when probabilities are multiplied, they harden into certainty. The size of the synthesis, its inexhaustible ability to assimilate fresh elements, and above all the deftness with which they are introduced all convince us that this is the system which was intended to be formed from the materials available.

The fact that Divine reserve is necessary has important consequences for the nature of the revelation. Newman asks us to 'consider in how mysterious a state all things are placed'. The wicked prosper, while the righteous suffer; this is a great temptation to unbelief; and it is to 'meet this difficulty that Almighty God has vouchsafed again and again to declare the unswerving rule of His government—favour to the obedient, punishment to the sinner'.[20] Of course, in the interests of clarity, Newman is forced to express himself with some clumsiness, when he speaks of Almighty God 'meeting a difficulty', as though He was blocking a loophole, but this only makes the point clearer. If the operation of the principle of reserve has,

[19] *P.S.* v. 9: 2 December 1838.
[20] *P.S.* iii. 104: 4 December 1831.

as it were, forced God to divulge the character of His government, then, unexpectedly enough, we are so much better off than we might have been.

Newman expressed his feeling that there were a variety of different revelations which might have been made in his sermon on *Mysteries in Religion,* when he wrote:

> And this, indeed, is an additional cause of thankfulness, that Almighty God has disclosed to us enough of His high Providence to raise such sacred and reverent feelings. Had He merely told us that He had pardoned us, we should have had overabundant cause for blessing and praising Him; but in showing us somewhat of the means, in vouchsafing to tell what cannot wholly be told, in condescending to abase heavenly things to the weak and stammering tongues of earth, He has enlarged our gratitude, yet sobered it with fear. (*P.S.* ii. 207: end of 1834)

Newman is so conscious of how much has been hidden, that he can imagine a case where even more might have been withheld. Thus he is acutely aware of the reasons which might be assigned for the fact that God made this particular revelation to us; in his sermon on *Infant Baptism* he tells us that none of us fully know our own condition, and that if we did, we would be too much overpowered to act:

> Did we see the complete consequences of any one sin, did we see how it spreads by the contagion of example and influence through the world, how many souls it injures, and what its external effects are, doubtless we should become speechless and motionless, as though we saw the flames of hell fire. Enough light is given us to direct us, and to make us responsible beings, not so much as to overwhelm us. We are not told the secret of our guilty nature, till we are told the means to escape from it; we are not told of God's fearful wrath, till we are told of His love in Christ. (*P.S.* iii. 295: 24 May 1835)

Newman achieves a balance between what is reserved and what revealed which is symmetrical; he investigates the consequences of the reserve which is employed by God, and finds (to use the necessarily crude terms of the model) that fine and delicate adjustments are made in the providential scheme, to compensate for and develop the effects of the principle of reserve.

From the consideration that God allows us enough light to direct ourselves, but not enough to overwhelm us, Newman proceeds to discuss particular consequences. In the sermon *Many called, few chosen*, he argues that since God keeps His counsels secret, we do not know whom He has chosen for salvation, so that 'while we understand this, and keep it before us, we shall not be puffed up about ourselves, nor harsh and censorious towards others . . .'[21]

In development of this, Newman finds that we are reserved from each other. When someone is introduced who is full of gifts, yet who does not appear to have his place in God's designs, there is a possibility that we might think more of the creature than the creator: 'it is a dangerous thing, it is too high a privilege, for sinners like ourselves, to know the best and innermost thoughts of God's servants. . . . The higher their gifts, the less fitted they are for being seen.'[22] Therefore many truths are sealed up from us.

Even the saints are given their place in the divine scheme because of the principle of reserve: 'So glorious and holy is our Lord, though viewed in His human nature, so perfect when He was tempted, so heavenly even upon earth, that sinners, such as we are, cannot endure the sight of Him at first.'[23] So, in mercy to us, He has included with His presence a great company of saints and angels in order to encourage and prepare us.

When God's reserved ways are considered, it becomes evident that the difficulties of faith are such that believers must be a small, exclusive body:

His marvellous providence works beneath a veil, which speaks but an untrue language; and to see Him who is the Truth and the Life, we must stoop underneath it, and so in our turn hide ourselves from the world. They who present themselves at kings' courts, pass on to the inner chambers, where the gaze of the rude multitude cannot

---

[21] *P.S.* v. 260: 10 September 1837.   [22] *P.S.* ii. 134: 25 March 1832.
[23] *P.S.* iii. 236: 14 September 1834.

pierce; and we, if we would see the King of kings in
His glory, must be content to disappear from the things
that are seen. Hid are the saints of God; . . . (*P.S.* ii. 9:
30 November 1830)

But this world is to be a 'world of practice and labour'; we are
only given glimpses of the Third Heaven to comfort us, but if
we indulge ourselves in them, rather than trying day by day to
purify ourselves for the future enjoyment of them, they become
'but a snare of our enemy'.[24]

Thus through his understanding of the principle of reserve,
Newman is able to limit man's situation and his capabilities,
to stress the sacredness of sacred things, and the reverence
which must be accorded them. Through his elucidation of the
principle, he can give us a 'sense of the utter nothingness
of worms such as we are; of our plain and absolute incapacity
to contemplate things *as they really are*; a perception of our
emptiness, before the great Vision of God; . . .'[25] And he can
give an idea of what sort of posture the Christian should adopt
before the unseen realities: 'the true Christian pierces through
the veil of this world and sees the next. He holds intercourse
with it; he addresses God, as a child might address his parent,
with as clear a view of Him, and with as unmixed a confidence in Him; with deep reverence indeed, and godly fear
and awe, but still with certainty and exactness. . . .'[26] The
reason, or things which are seen, are of no help; all that avails
is faith in things unseen. We should strain our eyes to make out
what God would have us do, and so Newman, unlike W. G.
Ward, was never worried by the problem of free will; he is
perfectly ready to postulate that God arbitrarily prohibits
certain actions or thoughts. In the sermon *Curiosity a Temptation to Sin*, he argues that because of curiosity, we 'intrude into
things forbidden, in various ways; in reading what we should
not read, in hearing what we should not hear, in seeing what
we should not see, in going into company whither we should
not go, in presumptuous reasonings and arguings when we
should have faith, in acting as if we were our own masters
where we should obey'.[27] For the truth is that we are not our

[24] *P.S.* ii. 367: 29 September 1831.   [25] *P.S.* ii. 209: end of 1834.
[26] *P.S.* vii. 211: 13 December 1829.   [27] *P.S.* viii. 64: 26 June 1831.

own masters, and should not act as if we were; man is confronted with very grave and serious duties and necessities, and his greatest need is to approve himself to his Maker. Thus he is not a free agent, and must follow God's will with the utmost scrupulousness. If God forbids him to do something which is apparently innocent, then he must obey unhesitatingly. Yet again, in this example, it can be seen how the idea that God withholds knowledge from us is closely related to all the ideas which are most characteristic of Newman.

Thus when Newman undertook, as his pastoral duty, to elucidate God's Providence, he appealed to the principle of reserve to sketch out the relative positions of God and man; with its help, he was able to indicate reserved areas of knowledge, and to skirt round them. Moreover, the principle proved fruitful in bringing various ideas and doctrines into systematic shape, thereby, in their symmetry, giving strength to the proofs of Christianity, and bringing it closer to the character which he gave of it twenty-five years later, when he wrote:

> I liken it to the mechanism of some triumph of skill, tower or spire, geometrical staircase, or vaulted roof, where 'Ars est celare artem:' where all display of strength is carefully avoided, and the weight is ingeniously thrown in a variety of directions, upon supports which are distinct from, or independent of each other. (*L. and D.* xix. 460)

Moreover, through Newman's handling of the principle of reserve, we understand the more fully what Keble meant when he sent off this criticism to Newman: 'I have always fancied that perhaps you were over sanguine in making things square, and did not quite allow enough for Bishop Butler's notion of doubt and intellectual difficulty being some men's element and appropriate trial.'[28] In the *Parochial Sermons*, Newman finds that the principle of reserve, which underlies all God's dealings with us, also accounts for the state of doubt and difficulty which we are in, and for him this is the next best thing to removing the doubts altogether. And so in this way Newman 'squares' the phenomena we perceive with the fundamental laws of Providence.

[28] *K.C.* 320.

CHAPTER FOUR

1. ECONOMY AS A MEANS TOWARDS CERTAINTY

So far, we have discussed the first applications of the principle of reserve, its employment during the Oxford Movement, and the way in which Newman drew out the principle in his *Sermons*. It remains to trace its more varied and esoteric manifestations. Here, where the principle is pursued to its limits, we find reserve running off into sacramentalism, conservatism, mystery, or simple restraint and taciturnity.

It has already been seen that the basis and pattern of reserve lies in the inability of the finite human mind to comprehend the infinite divine realities. One of the great problems is how what is unknown to human experience may be represented. Clearly, exact representation is impossible, but it is worth while, and even necessary, that some representation be attempted. Since Newman believed in the existence of unseen realities, the problem was particularly acute for him, and one with which he grappled throughout his life. The word he chose to convey the idea of partial representation was 'economy', a word which, although used by the Fathers to express a prudent husbandry, is attributed to Newman himself by the *Oxford English Dictionary*. He first drew out the implications of this idea in the *Arians of the Fourth Century*, where he wrote that the word economy might be used for the general system of Providence or for the work of creation, as opposed to the absolute perfection of God. Then he goes on to say, that 'since this everlasting and unchangeable quiescence is the simplest and truest notion we can obtain of the Deity, it seems to follow, that strictly speaking, all those so-called Economies or dispensations, which display His character in action, are but condescensions to the infirmity and peculiarity of our minds, shadowy representations of realities which are incomprehensible to creatures such as ourselves. . . .'[1] Hence general

---

[1] *Ari.* 75.

moral laws are but an 'Economia' of greater truths untold, 'the best practical communication of them which our minds in their present state will admit'. The phenomena of the external world are a divine mode of conveying to the mind the realities of existence. In this passage we observe that tendency, which is so pronounced in Newman, to regard things, not as sufficient in themselves, and existing solely by themselves, but as possessing untold possibilities and depths. Because a vast gulf lies between God and ourselves, the world and material things are moved into the gap as a means of approximating to the realities which lie on the other side, invisible to us.

Newman discussed his theory of the economy in greater detail in his University Sermon on *Developments in Religious Doctrine*; we teach children by accommodations, and teach them the most perfect truth, 'that is, the nearest approach to truth, compatible with their condition'.[2] Many ideas cannot be exactly expressed in language, and so some expedient or economy must be employed. Again, many people divide and subdivide that world of ideas which come before them on different principles: 'They seem ever to be dodging each other, and need a common measure or economy to mediate between them.'[3] Fables are economies, and mathematical science also affords many examples of this principle; in the same way, music is a representation of something greater: 'Those mysterious stirrings of heart, and keen emotions . . . have escaped from some higher sphere; they are the outpourings of eternal harmony in the medium of created sound. . . .'[4]

If everything is an economy of something more real than itself in the realm of Ideas, then we are firmly within the Platonic tradition, and indeed it was seen in the first chapter that the idea of God upon which the principle of reserve is based was strongly influenced by Plato. This tells us something about Newman's mind, which will be discussed further in the next chapter; more immediately, it tells us something about his attitude to Truth; as he says in a letter to Samuel Wilberforce in 1835, 'In truth we arrive at truth by *approximations*.'[5] The

    [2] *U.S.* 341: 2 February 1843.   [3] *U.S.* 342.   [4] *U.S.* 346.
    [5] David Newsome, 'Justification and Sanctification: Newman and the Evangelicals', *Journal of Theological Studies*, New Series, Vol xv, 1964, p. 42, dated

word 'approximate' can carry us far; in the *Grammar of Assent*, Newman wrote: '. . . in science we sometimes use a definition or a *formula*, not as exact, but as being sufficient for our purpose, for working out certain conclusions, for a practical approximation, the error being small, till a certain point is reached. This is what in theological investigations I should call an economy. . . .'[6] Thus the words or definition are roughly equivalent to the reality they represent. It is not exact, but it is sufficient. When reserve is practised, and knowledge is withheld, and disclosed only gradually, the position at the beginning is only a rough approximation to reality, but as the process is continued, the representation, or economy, arrives at the truth. Put this way, it is clear that this concept is analogous to the method of the Differential Calculus in mathematics, and indeed in 1862 we find Newman proposing to read a book on the differential calculus, 'as the philosophy of that subject is a point about which I have great interest'.[7]

Here we may detect another instance of Newman's debt to the Oriel Common Room, and to Whately in particular. In his *Rhetoric*, Whately speaks of several testimonies producing a degree of probability far exceeding the sum of their several forces, and goes on to consider the case where we cannot obtain direct proof, but we may '*gradually approach* indefinitely near to the case supposed'.[8] Whately takes the laws of motion as an illustration; they suppose that once a body is set in motion, it will continue with uniform velocity. We know that a body projected along a rough surface is soon stopped, while a body along ice will continue far longer. Thus by means of such approximations, we can conceive of cases where the body will conform precisely to the laws of motion. Davison, too, relies upon cumulative arguments, 'for though some kind of proof be incapable of accession by an extended cumulative reason, the proof of religion is not of that nature, but one which gathers light and strength by the concentrated force of all its

---

29 January 1835. James Stephen, to whom Wilberforce forwarded it, was rather shocked at the idea that certainty could be attained at all.

[6] *An Essay in Aid of a Grammar of Assent*, London, 1881, p. 47.

[7] *L. and D.* xx. 226.

[8] Richard Whately, *Elements of Rhetoric. Comprising the Substance of an Article in the Encyclopaedia Metropolitana*, Oxford, 1828, p. 56.

moral evidence.'[9] In fact, very much later in life, Newman refers his correspondent to 'what Mr. Davison calls a *cumulative* argument',[10] and so it is probable that these two men first introduced Newman to approximations and converging probabilities.

Newman employs the language of the calculus quite strikingly; there is a remarkable example in the *Development of Christian Doctrine*, when he says: '. . . whole objects do not create in the intellect whole ideas, but are, to use a mathematical phrase, thrown into series, into a number of statements, strengthening, interpreting, correcting each other, and with more or less exactness approximating, as they accumulate, to a perfect image.'[11] As well as the words 'approximating', and 'limits', we frequently find Newman using the word 'tending' to describe the way in which imperfect representations gradually approach the truth. Thus we see that for Newman, each thing is separate from anything else; the essence of a thing only discloses itself slowly and imperfectly. The fullest expression of this is in the *Parochial Sermons*, where, in a most striking passage, he asks us to survey some populous town; after a vivid description of the life and energy of the place, he goes on:

> But what is the truth? why, that every being in that great concourse is his own centre, and all things about him are but shades, but a 'vain shadow,' in which he 'walketh and disquieteth himself in vain.' He has his own hopes and fears, desires, judgments, and aims; he is everything to himself, and no one else is really anything. No one outside of him can really touch him, can touch his soul, his immortality; he must live with himself for ever. He has a depth within him unfathomable, an infinite abyss of existence; and the scene in which he bears part for the moment is but like a gleam of sunshine upon its surface. (*P.S.* iv. 82: 27 March 1836)

The essence of each person and thing is hidden from us, and one of the great problems is how this elusive essence is to be communicated, once it is detected, and throughout his life

[9] John Davison, *Discourses on Prophecy, in which are considered its Structure, Use, and Inspiration*, London, 1825, p. 24.

[10] *L. and D.* xxiv. 145.

[11] *An Essay on the Development of Christian Doctrine*, London, 1876, p. 55.

Newman felt that economies, or approximations, were the only possible way. In 1859 he received a stimulus which led him to develop his ideas more fully. Mansel published his *Limits of Religious Thought* in 1858, which was reviewed by Simpson in the *Rambler* in December 1858. Simpson argued that Mansel owed much to Newman, but had not acknowledged his debt; Mansel denied that a debt had ever existed, and asserted that he had not read much of Newman's writings. Charles Meynell raised this question with Newman, who replied that he had read enough of Mansel's book to show him that he agreed with it. But he went on to say: 'Nay it seems to me taken from my own Protestant teaching. This does not hinder me from feeling a serious objection and fear of some things which he has said.'[12] After this, Newman wrote, apparently at breakneck speed, in handwriting which is at times scarcely legible, a short treatise on economy, which was in the end not sent to Meynell. The motive he gives for writing is that Mansel's doctrine had met with opposition from Protestant divines, which made him anxious, since Mansel had quoted from him at one point. In a passage of great interest, Newman acknowledges that Mansel's word 'regulative' means the same as his 'economical': 'My own word from first to last has been economical, as I have explained it especially in my book on the Arians.'[13] The first example he gives is of truth as far as it goes, but not the whole truth, and illustrates it with the story of a child explaining to another that 'Bonaparte was a naughty man, who took all the toys of little Boys— which was quite true.' The next example is of undefined or indistinct truth, and he instances parables, where we do not know 'how far and to what limit the images employed represent the truth revealed to us'. Newman's next example is of 'Instances of approximation to the truth by various images correcting each other', and he shows how the various images of Christ, if taken separately, lead to Sabellianism or Arianism, but 'if taken together, they limit each other.'

The fourth example which Newman gives is where one definite image is taken, so that 'we have to discover by reason or by external teaching the point of the analogy', and instances

[12] *L. and D.* xix. 256.
[13] Newman Archives, Birmingham Oratory, vol. lxxiv, dated 20 December 1859.

the blind man who is told that scarlet is like the sound of the trumpet, and also the way in which Scripture language concerning God's wrath or jealousy conveys to us 'ideas of states of mind which we cannot possibly dissociate from human imperfections'. Then he argues that 'the view of nature irresistibly leads us to the notion of design', but that it is difficult to support this argument on strictly philosophical grounds, and that therefore, those who believe in God for this reason 'believe on a wrong basis'; thus, he concludes, 'an uncertain or unsound argument leads to a right conclusion.' He insists that what is told is true objectively, but is not true in 'that nearest approach to truth which our intellect can arrive at', and remarks that this method is intended to try the separate hearts to which it is presented. He ends the treatise with a disquisition on the senses; each modifies the other, and none of the senses would lead us to imagine the existence of the others, so that in effect it is perfectly possible that there are other senses with which we have not been endowed.

In this little treatise, Newman set out his theory of economy in the most systematic form it ever achieved. It is a theory which maintains on the one hand the existence of Objective Truth, while on the other asserting that our vision of it is imperfect. Such a theory demands a clear understanding of the means by which knowledge is communicated; it sees that there must be a medium of communication, and that this medium must colour the knowledge which it transmits. For this reason, it is possible to estimate the amount of distortion which the truth suffers when it undergoes this process.

Shortly after he wrote this treatise, Newman made his most strenuous, and certainly most remarkable, attempt to throw the truths which are usually expressed in one medium into another calculus.[14] In an entry in the *Philosophical Notebook*, dated March 1860, we find him working at this problem:

> Fluxions then constitute an economical method, representing the truths, existing in differentials, in a calculus of which space and motion in space is the basis.
> This somewhat represents what I would hold of sensible

[14] Cf. Moz. ii. 97: Gladstone 'was obliged to speak in the language, or according to the calculus, of the Commons'.

phenomena as contrasted with the real essences from which they issue and on which they depend.

2. And so geometry is an economical representation of algebraical science or of some science unknown deeper still. . . .[15]

We note again Newman's readiness to throw reality back one stage, and to suggest that what everyone else takes for reality is merely a representation of reality. But more remarkable still is the passage where he uses mathematics to illustrate something which we frequently find him saying in the *Sermons*: that, to our imperfect vision, one truth may seem to contradict another. And so he begins: 'State it thus for clearness:

$$M = a - b - x + y/^3$$

Where M is a real quantity or substance, say 100 tons of lead. . . .'[16] He proceeds to expand this expression according to the Binomial Theorem, and summarizes his conclusions as follows:

Put in shape the points to be insisted on in page opposite
1. that the expression has a LAW. This I have not mentioned For it is the law of the binomial theorem.
2. Yet it seems *most confused* and lawless.
3. that quantities disappear in one term and start up in another when the whole varies in magnitude, or the terms vary
4. that it is often impossible to give the real essence which this or that term represents—some combinations of letters seeming to have no meaning.[17]

This is a demonstration of the difference between appearance and reality, for what appears to be lawless is actually ruled by the strictest mathematical laws. Thus Newman shows that if we are living among symbols, imperfect representations of reality beyond our knowledge, then we may be deluded by the appearance. Indeed, the contrast between appearance and reality was of constant interest to Newman, as may be seen from the letter in which he told his correspondent how interest-

[15] *The Philosophical Notebook of John Henry Newman*, ed. at the Birmingham Oratory by E. Sillem, Louvain, 1970, p. 111.
[16] Ibid., p. 112. [17] Ibid., p. 114.

ing he found the 'ten thousand little details and complications of daily life and family history', and how evanescent they apparently were. Then he asked:

> Is there any record of them preserved anywhere, any more than of the fall of the leaves in Autumn? or are they themselves some reflexion, as in an earthly mirror, of some greater truths above? So I think of musical sounds and their combinations—they are momentary—but is it not some momentary opening and closing of the Veil which hangs between the worlds of spirit and sense? (*L. and D.* xix. 415)

He was constantly aware that the eye saw only the surface, and that there were infinite depths and possibilities beyond. We are accustomed to speak of Newman as possessing two sides; on the one hand we speak of the sceptical temperament, which is unable to take things for things, and which thinks that understanding and communication are practically impossible. On the other hand, there is the side of which Keble was thinking when he wrote: 'I have always fancied that perhaps you were over sanguine in making things square. . . .'[18] When he tries to make things square he is the logician who advances confidently towards certainty, for whom approximations approximate towards truth. It seems, then, that for Newman the differential calculus was a means of uniting these two sides; it enabled him to use symbols approximating to the elusive essence of things in order to attain to that certainty for which he strove. And, astonishingly enough, this is precisely the method of the *Grammar of Assent*. We usually approach the *Grammar of Assent* from the direction from which Newman himself approached it, that is, from empirical psychology, the idea that people act, not on demonstrative certainty, but on moral certainty, where probabilities harden into certainty. But we have just approached from the direction of mathematics, and can see that it is as easy to say, in the manner of the calculus, that cumulative probabilities *approximate* to certainty. As we have seen in the *Arians*, Newman employed this method of approximation from a very early period, and that the word 'economy' is to epistemology what the words 'differential calculus' are to mathematics.

[18] *K.C.* 320.

ii. THE VARIOUS MANIFESTATIONS OF RESERVE IN NEWMAN'S WRITINGS

Since we are at a distance from truth, and can only apprehend it by means of economical representations, words themselves are economies. Thus Newman writes in the *University Sermons*:

> It is hardly too much to say, that almost all reasons formally adduced in moral inquiries, are rather specimens and symbols of the real grounds, than those grounds themselves. They do but approximate to a representation of the general character of the proof which the writer wishes to convey to another's mind . . . they are hints towards, and samples of, the true reasoning, and demand an active, ready, candid, and docile mind, which can throw itself into what is said, neglect verbal difficulties, and pursue and carry out principles. (*U.S.* 275: 29 June 1840)

Words do not transmit the essence, but afford a partial insight into truth; they demand the participation of the reader, in a way which reminds us of what Newman says so many times, that one cannot expect to be *made* to believe, but that belief must come through trying to believe.

The nature of words has further important consequences for those who endeavour to spread religion by means of arguments; truths can never be expressed properly, and so in the *Lectures on Justification*, after explaining that words cannot give a real apprehension of Christ, Newman goes on to say that the doctrines will never appear to advantage, 'or be described with justice, in controversy, which employs the language of the unregenerate. It is true its maintainers *have* attempted to argue and refute their opponents, but to do so was a mistake. . . .'[19] In this way reserve is imposed on religious men, for even if they did wish to expose their most sacred doctrines, words would be too clumsy to communicate them. Hence, too, words are the cause of unreality in religious controversy; in the *University Sermons*, Newman asserts that frequently we

---

[19] *Lectures on the Doctrine of Justification*, London, 1874, p. 15.

do not recognize our sensations and ideas, however carefully they are put into words: 'The representation seems out of shape and strange, and startles us, even though we know not how to find fault with it.'[20] He goes on to say:

> This difficulty of analyzing our most recondite feelings happily and convincingly, has a most important influence upon the science of the Evidences. Defenders of Christianity naturally select as reasons for belief, not the highest, the truest, the most sacred, the most intimately persuasive, but such as best admit of being exhibited in argument; and these are commonly not the real reasons in the case of religious men. (*U.S.* 270)

And not only is there unreality in argument as a result of the deficiencies of words, but the arguments themselves are not even convincing; earlier in the *University Sermons* he had written: '. . . still, let it be inquired whether these Evidences are not rather to be viewed as splendid philosophical investigations than practical arguments; at best bulwarks intended for overawing the enemy by their strength and number, rather than for actual use in war.'[21] Words so little, effectively, represent the ideas and substances they stand for, that argument is actually unnecessary, as we see from this letter of the Catholic period:

> . . . the utmost I aspire to do is to effect 'a first approximation to the required solution'. This has been my feeling both when I wrote of Development of doctrine and of University Education. Another point is this, that I rather undervalue cut and dried arguments, though I do not say so, and think that statement to most persons is proof—(i.e. directly a mind takes in what is meant, a true view elicits from the mind proofs of itself by its own vigour). I have expressed this at the end of one of my University Sermons. 'If I succeed in defining etc I shall be content, without attempting to defend . . . When men understand what each other mean, they see, for the most part, that controversy is either superfluous or hopeless.' (*L. and D.* xv. 381)

---

[20] *U.S.* 270.   [21] *U.S.* 65: 11 December 1831.

This line of discussion leads directly back to one of the first aims of the Oxford Movement. It had been proposed that changes should be made in the Liturgy, and the Tractarians rose in its defence. If the words were not of precisely ascertained meaning, any change might entail the destruction of treasures of which we had no conception. Thus when Newman sets out in the *Parochial Sermons* the feelings which he thinks we ought to have on our minds, we find among them

> a conviction, that what is put before us, in nature or in grace, though true in such a full sense that we dare not tamper with it, yet is but an intimation useful for particular purposes, useful for practice, useful in its department, 'until the day-break and the shadows flee away', useful in such a way that both the one and the other representation may at once be used, as two languages, as two separate approximations towards the Awful Unknown Truth, such as will not mislead us in their respective provinces. (*P.S.* ii. 209: end of 1834)

Therefore we must not tamper with what we do not understand:

> Christ is within the veil. We must not search curiously what is His present office, what is meant by His pleading His sacrifice, and by His perpetual intercession for us. And, since we do not know, we will studiously keep to the figure given us in Scripture: we will not attempt to interpret it, or change the wording of it, being wise above what is written. We will not neglect it, because we do not understand it. We will hold it as a Mystery. . . . (*P.S.* ii. 211)

And so the conclusion he reaches is that we should 'jealously maintain this, and every other portion of our Creed, lest, by dropping jot or tittle, we suffer the truths concealed therein to escape from us'.[22] It is noticeable here how Newman employs the language which is usually associated with the principle of reserve; moreover, the principle is consistently utilized to connect various phenomena.

The discussion has so far touched upon the defective nature of language, and also upon its sacramental nature. It is now

[22] *P.S.* ii. 213.

time to speak of the pregnant aspects of language. Just as the Anglican formularies preserved Catholic truth, only revealing it to him who looked for it, words possess hidden riches, which are gradually unfolded to the seeker:

> Revelation, as a Manifestation, is a doctrine variously received by various minds, but nothing more to each than that which each mind comprehends it to be. Considered as a Mystery, it is a doctrine enunciated by inspiration, in human language, as the only possible medium of it, and suitably, according to the capacity of language; a doctrine *lying hid* in language, to be received in that language from the first by every mind, whatever be its separate power of understanding it; entered into more or less by this or that mind, as it may be; and admitting of being apprehended more and more perfectly according to the diligence of this mind and that. It is one and the same, independent and real, of depth unfathomable, and illimitable in its extent.[23]

This extract initiates a train of thought in which we pass from language to the way in which the mind operates. If there is in thought a sequence from A to Z, where Z represents a fuller possession of the truth than A, then it is plain that this fulfils all the criteria of the principle of reserve, in that one arrives at a more complete truth by means of a gradual progression. This is the way in which the mind reaches a fuller understanding of each truth, and slowly consolidates its hold upon it; moreover, it is the way in which God communicates knowledge to us:

> This is His gracious way with us: He gives, not all at once, but by measure and season, wisely. To him that hath, more shall be given. But we must begin at the beginning. Each truth has its own order; we cannot join the way of life at any point of the course we please; we cannot learn advanced truths before we have learned primary ones. (*P.S.* viii. 195: 17 October 1830)

Thus, where we spoke before of the attempts of words to represent essences, we now speak of the way in which essences disclose themselves to the mind's perception. This may happen

---

[23] *Essays Critical and Historical*, London, 1881, i. 41.

almost casually: '. . . we may be in the practice of reading Scripture carefully, and trying to serve God, and its sense may, as if suddenly, break upon us, in a way it never did before. Some thought may suggest itself to us, which is a key to a great deal in Scripture, or which suggests a great many other thoughts.'[24] This new insight may enable us to 'enter into the life of the early Christians, as recorded in Scripture, which before was hidden from us'.

Or it may happen that the essence discloses itself as the result of the experience of years: 'Passages [of the classics], which to a boy are but rhetorical commonplaces . . . at length come home to him, when long years have passed, and he has had experience of life, and pierce him, as if he had never before known them, with their sad earnestness and vivid exactness.'[25] The experience given by the world illustrates classical authors in the same way as the religious sense gains knowledge of Holy Scripture.

By means of this process, the mind wins a fuller under-standing for itself; as Newman says:

> . . . the image of God, if duly cherished, may expand, deepen, and be completed, with the growth of their powers and in the course of life, under the varied lessons, within and without them, which are brought home to them con-cerning that same God, One and Personal, by means of education, social intercourse, experience, and literature. (*G.A.* 116)

It is important to note his use of such phrases as 'duly cherished', or 'carefully cultivated'; fuller knowledge belongs only to one who is initiated, and who in consequence receives the dis-closure of the completer truth. As Newman puts it in the *Parochial Sermons*: 'God gives second and third gifts to those

---

[24] *P.S.* viii. 29: 27 October 1839.

[25] *G.A.* 78. Cf. *V.M.* i. 154: ' It is very observable how a latent prejudice can act in obscuring or rather annihilating certain passages of Scripture in the mental vision . . . . A man perhaps is in the habit of reading Scripture for years, and has no impression whatever produced upon his mind by such portions of it as speak of God's free grace, and the need of spiritual aid. These are at length suddenly and forcibly brought home to him; and then perhaps he changes his religious views altogether, and declares that Scripture has hitherto been to him nothing better than a sealed book.'

who improve the first; let us improve the first, and then we know not how high may be the spiritual faculties which at length He will give us. Who is there, who, on setting out on a journey, sees before him his destination?'[26] Since religious truth is hidden from us, we must engage to let ourselves be carried forward, humbly and tractably, towards the greater truth. Newman expresses this, when he writes that every word of revelation has a deep meaning, and is a mystery or sacrament, and goes on to say:

> We may read it, confess it, but there is something in it which we cannot fathom, which we only, more or less, as the case may be, not perfectly, enter into. Accordingly, when a candidate for Baptism repeats the Articles of the Creed, he is confessing something incomprehensible in its depth, and indefinite in its extent. He cannot know at the time what he is binding on himself, whither he is letting himself be carried. (*V.M.* i. 257)

This is a theme which Newman repeats many times, that one must make trial for the sake of truth, and that one must give oneself generously to the pursuit of truth; if God is hidden, and portions of knowledge are withheld from us, then we must have faith to be sure that what we cannot see actually does exist. To have faith is to grasp firmly the portion of truth allotted one, as well as to perceive the relationship between Revealed and Unrevealed Truth. Thus Newman says that

> To believe in Objective Truth is to throw ourselves forward upon that which we have but partially mastered or made subjective; to embrace, maintain, and use general propositions which are larger than our own capacity, of which we cannot see the bottom, which we cannot follow out into their multiform details; to come before and bow before the import of such propositions, as if we were contemplating what is real and independent of human judgment. (*Ess.* i. 34)

This forward progress and advance is strongly reminiscent of the Development of Doctrine, and a direct link may be traced

[26] *P.S.* vi. 33: 21 March 1841.

between the theory of development and the principle of reserve. Newman wrote that 'to me the words "development in dogma" are substantially nothing but the process by which, under the magisterium of the Church, implicit faith becomes explicit.'[27] The doctrines which had been kept hidden and reserved are brought forward and set down in writing, and Newman draws out this process clearly in the *Historical Sketches*: the oracles of divine truth repeat the same message, but as time goes on 'they utter it with greater force and precision, under diverse forms, with fuller luminousness, and a richer ministration of thought, statement, and argument.' They adapt themselves to meet the different needs of each age:

> They cautiously reserve their new enunciation of the old Truth, till it is imperatively demanded. And, as it happens in kings' cabinets, that surmises arise, and rumours spread, of what is said in council, and is in course of preparation, and secrets perhaps get wind, true in substance or in direction, though distorted in detail; so too, before the Church speaks, one or other of her forward children speaks for her, and, while he does anticipate to a certain point what she is about to say or enjoin, he states it incorrectly, makes it error instead of truth, and risks his own faith in the process.[28]

It is remarkable that the way in which the Church apprehends the truth is one of approximation, whereby the truth is gradually wrought out of error; the course of events slowly brings it out into the open.

Just as the individual gains a clearer view of what he holds, and gradually sees further and further, the Church finds out what it holds, and gradually, as events demand it, discloses what had formerly lain hidden and implicit within its bosom. Newman confirms that this link between development and reserve exists when he writes that he would like to say that the Church apprehends it more clearly, and almost thinks 'that Bossuet countenances such a notion'.[29]

We are led on step by step, then, until we attain the full truth. This process begins with the Notes of the Church. Those who approach Newman by way of the *Apologia pro Vita*

[27] *L. and D.* xx. 224.   [28] *Historical Sketches*, London, 1872, i. 192 f.
[29] *L. and D.* xx. 224.

Sua are often surprised at the way he uses the 'look' of things to reach his conclusion; if the Anglican Church is in the position of the Donatists, for example, why should the other consequences follow from this? But the Fathers, and Newman, held that 'the "look" of things was ever meant to be a providential note, in order to *save* argument.' Thus when Dr. Wiseman maintained that St. Austin or St. Basil would hold that Rome was the Catholic Church, while the Anglicans were the heretics, Newman was forced to confess that 'I cannot deny either of his positions—that the Father *would* at *first sight* so judge of us—or that they (the Fathers) did so teach.'[30] In accordance with this method of judging by the 'look' of things is his theory of the Notes of the Church; he held that the Church bore on her forehead signs and tokens to show where the true Church was to be found, in the same way that shops put out signs. The four Notes of the Church are Catholicity, Apostolicity, Unity, and Sanctity, which Newman explained in his volume of *Sermons on Subjects of the Day* as follows:

> Christ, in mercy to all who seek Him, has been accustomed in all ages, in anticipation of His true inward witness, to hold forth certain plain and general tokens of His Presence, to show the world where He is to be found. These are for beginners; or for those who are not yet beginners, that they *may* begin, and may thus be led on by such experience of His grace, to discern those holier and better notes of which He speaks in the text. (*S.D.* 318: 28 November 1841)

If the Notes of the Church lead us to the Church, then the Church leads us to God, for the Church is the visible representation of God. Newman expresses this thought in the *Parochial Sermons*, when he says 'well then may the Church be called invisible', since the Holy Spirit and the Church and her true children on earth cannot be ascertained by mortal eye. Then he continues:

> . . . had God so willed, she might have had no visible tokens at all of her existence, and been as entirely and absolutely hidden from us as the Holy Ghost is, her Lord and Governor.

---

[30] Newman Archives, Birmingham Oratory, vol. xcviii, J. H. Newman to J. W. Bowden, dated 21 February 1840.

But seeing that the Holy Ghost is our life, so that to gain life we must approach Him, in mercy to us, His place of abode, the Church of the Living God, is not so utterly veiled from our eyes as He is; but He has given us certain outward signs, as tokens for knowing, and means for entering that living Shrine in which He dwells. (*P.S.* iv. 172 f.: 14 May 1837)

Thus the catechumen recognizes the Church by means of the Notes, and is then led forward by means of a series of gradations; the theory of Notes is therefore complementary to the idea that God is hidden, since without them it would be impossible to recognize His Presence on earth, and so the beginner would never get started on his way.

III. THE ARGUMENT FROM ANTECEDENT PROBABILITY

Since the evidence which can be adduced on behalf of religion is imperfect, some logical and rhetorical means must be devised for using what has been given us to establish what has been withheld from us. Newman expressed this when, six years before his death, he advised Wilfrid Ward to be very particular in pressing on the attention of the young men the *nature* of the proof they were to expect on religious subjects, going on to say:

They must not expect too much. Butler somewhere compares the imperfection of the religious argument to the imperfection of a ruined castle. In many cases the shape of the castle is quite as clearly determined by the ruin which remains as it would be were the castle whole. And so with the proofs of natural and revealed religion. There is enough capable of expression to indicate the *shape* and *character* of the proof, though it is in detail very imperfect. (Ward ii. 495)

The method which Newman adopted for proceeding from the known to the unknown was the Argument from Antecedent Probability, and we may gain some idea of the importance which Newman attached to it from this letter of 1853: 'Again, I *stand by* my (Oxford) University Discourses . . . and am almost a zealot for their substantial truth—and if I have brought out one truth in any thing I have written, I consider it to be the *importance of antecedent probability* in conviction. It is how you convert factory girls as well as philosophers...'[31] At another time he wrote that, for the positive proof of Catholicism, he rested the argument on antecedent probabilities or *verisimilia*, 'which are to my mind most powerful, (and practically sufficient for they are in fact the Notes of The Church) . . .'[32]

Simply expressed, an antecedent probability is what we may expect from the state of the case, and from *a priori* considerations. It depends either on the knowledge we have gained from experience, or from analogy, and must always be reinforced by an examination of what actually and historically happened. Perhaps the most concise demonstration of this connection between expectation and event is to be found when Newman wrote: 'Next, passing from antecedent probabilities to history . . .'[33]

Assuming for the moment what it is scarcely necessary to prove, that the phrase antecedent probability is highly characteristic of Newman, it is curious to ascertain the source whence he derived the argument. There can be little doubt that it represents part of Newman's debt to Richard Whately, which was acknowledged in general terms in the *Apologia*.[34] In a letter, he wrote that Whately was the first person who opened his mind, 'that is, who gave it ideas and principles to cogitate upon. He showed me some MS dialogues of his on Logic, to me quite a new subject, for I had despised it; I copied them out; and then he proposed to me . . . to turn them into the shape of a treatise for the Encyclopedia Metropolitana.'[35]

Whately put his thoughts on antecedent probability into systematic shape in his *Elements of Rhetoric*, which also appeared in the *Encyclopedia Metropolitana*, and which was printed in book form in 1828. He records in the Preface that 'a brief outline of the principal part of the . . . Work was sketched

[31] *L. and D.* xv. 381.   [32] Ibid., xiii. 319.   [33] Ibid., xxiv. 7.
[34] *Apo.* 23.   [35] *L. and D.* xv. 176.

out several years ago for the private use of some young friends,'[36] and it is probable that Newman first came upon the argument in this manuscript, or in conversation with Whately.

In the chapters dealing with conviction, Whately first distinguishes between arguments 'a priori', or 'antecedent probability',[37] and 'a posteriori', denominating the latter the 'Body of evidence'. He warns that the phrase ' "*a priori*" Argument . . . would however generally be understood to extend to any argument drawn from an *antecedent* or *forerunner*, whether a *Cause* or not.'[38]

That established, we next come across a passage of considerable interest:

> When arguments of each of the two formerly-mentioned classes are employed, those from Cause to Effect (Antecedent-probability) have usually the precedence.
>
> Men are apt to listen with prejudice to the Arguments which are adduced to prove any thing which appears *abstractedly* improbable; i.e. according to what has been above laid down, *unnatural*, or (if such an expression might be allowed) *unplausible*; and this prejudice is to be removed by the Argument from Cause to Effect, which thus prepares the way for the reception of the other Arguments; e.g. if a man who bore a good character were accused of corruption, the strongest evidence against him might avail little; but if he were proved to be of a covetous disposition, this, though it would not alone be allowed to substantiate the crime, would have great weight in inducing his judges to lend an ear to the evidence. And thus, in what relates to the future also, the *a priori* Argument and Example support each other, when thus used in conjunction, and in the order prescribed . . .[39]

Further, we find that Whately gives an example of this method of reasoning, and points out how it has the effect of preparing the mind for other arguments, to which it would otherwise be closed:

> E.g. in the statement of the Evidences of our Religion, so as to give them their just weight, much depends on the

---

[36] Richard Whately, *Elements of Rhetoric*, Oxford, 1828, p. i.
[37] Ibid., p. 40 n. 1.   [38] Ibid., p. 41.   [39] Ibid., pp. 81 f.

Order in which they are placed. The Antecedent probability that a Revelation should be given to man, and that it should be established by miracles, all would allow to be, considered by itself, in the absence of strong direct testimony, utterly insufficient to establish the Conclusion. On the other hand, miracles considered abstractedly, as represented to have occurred without any occasion or reason for them being assigned, carry with them such a strong intrinsic improbability as could not be wholly surmounted even by such evidence as would fully establish any other matters of fact. But the evidences of the former class, however inefficient alone towards the establishment of the Conclusion, have very great weight in preparing the mind for receiving the other Arguments; which again, though they would be listened to with prejudice if not so supported, will then be allowed their just weight.[40]

The importance of the argument from antecedent probability is confirmed by the method employed by Bishop Butler, who relied upon the presumption afforded by the analogy of nature, and it is noticeable that on several occasions Newman uses 'presumption' as a synonym for 'antecedent probability'. Further, other members of the Oriel Common Room may have exerted an influence in the same direction on him; Davison begins his *Discourses on Prophecy* with an Introduction dealing with the previous probability of a Divine Revelation,[41] while Copleston includes a long section on Analogy in his *Enquiry into the Doctrines of Necessity and Predestination*, a work which has already been mentioned in the first chapter. Further, it is stressed in Whately's edition of a *Discourse on Predestination* that such methods of attaining to knowledge are necessary from the imperfection of our faculties; God is the object of none of our senses, and if we know anything of Him at all, 'it must be by deductions of reason, by analogy and comparison, by resembling him to something that we do know and are acquainted with.'[42] At all events, it is clear that his colleagues would have accustomed him to presumptive reason-

---

[40] Ibid., p. 84.

[41] John Davison, *Discourses on Prophecy, in which are considered its Structure, Use, and Inspiration*, London, 1825, p. 1.

[42] *Discourse on Predestination*, ed. by Richard Whately, Oxford, 1821, p. 21.

ings, and that conditions in the Oriel Common Room were propitious for Newman to acquire the habit of asking what might be expected to happen, and then ascertaining if the expectation had been borne out by the event.

Indeed, we can trace the development of Newman's mind; while in 1820 he noted that 'A priori arguments seem to me the most fallacious of the fallacious',[43] we next find him in August 1823 recording that his brother Charles had argued the antecedent improbability of eternal punishment, evidently turning his brother's newly acquired logical weapon against himself.[44] Then in a review of *Duncan's Travels* in the *British Review* of May 1824, and attributed to Newman by Fr. H. Tristram, the writer feels it 'antecedently improbable that America will excel in this branch of learning'.[45] The argument appears in each of the articles written for the *Encyclopedia Metropolitana*; the Cicero, finished May 1824, and Apollonius Tyanaeus and Miracles, finished January 1826. The section on miracles contains an argument as to the antecedent credibility of a miracle, against Hume's view, and in fact Newman refers the reader to Whately's treatise on rhetoric.

In 1826 Thomas Mozley gave the following account of his first week under Newman's tuition, which shows how Newman had absorbed Whately's method of reasoning:

> I have at last had an interview with my new tutor, Mr. Newman, who gave me much good advice on the subject of themes, and gave me a manuscript treatise on composition written by Whately, who is a famous man here. This I have copied, and have all the week been furiously engaged in causes and effects and antecedent probabilities and plausibilities, which, as I have never read a line of logic, have been very abstruse. (Moz. i. 131)

Since he had adopted this method of reasoning with such alacrity, it is probable that Newman realized that the argument from antecedent probability offered several important advantages. It allowed the state of the evidence and the strength of presumptions in favour of any statement to be put

---

[43] *A.W.* 164.   [44] *A.W.* 192.
[45] 'Duncan's Travels', *British Review and London Critical Journal*, vol. xxii, no. 44, May 1824, p. 160. The attribution is in *Apo.* 493. Cf. *A.W.* 195.

forth with considerable clarity, and it demonstrated forcibly that if we are satisfied to use antecedent probability as a matter of course in our daily life, then we have no cause to demand more rigorous proof for reasonings on religious subjects. Further, as Whately had pointed out in his *Rhetoric*, the use of antecedent probability will lead the prejudiced reader to admit that some proposition is probable, in which case he is more likely to be receptive to the body of proof.

While Newman continued to employ antecedent arguments in his writings, it was not until 1839, in his University Sermon on *Faith and Reason contrasted as Habits of Mind* that he brought out the importance of antecedent probability in conviction. In this sermon Newman argues that Faith does not demand evidence so strong as is necessary for what is commonly considered a rational conviction,

> because it is mainly swayed by antecedent considerations. In this way it is, that the two principles are opposed to one another: Faith is influenced by previous notices, prepossessions, and (in a good sense of the word) prejudices; but Reason, by direct and definite proof. The mind that believes is acted upon by its own hopes, fears, and existing opinions; whereas it is supposed to reason severely, when it rejects antecedent proof of a fact,—rejects everything but the actual evidence producible in its favour. (*U.S.* 187 ff.: 6 January 1839)

Newman next shows that no one reasons severely in everyday life: 'Faith is a principle of action, and action does not allow time for minute and finished investigations.' He maintains that the principle behind the workings of the mind is that 'we do not call for evidence till antecedent probabilities fail.' In daily life, each of us sees that we do not have all the information which is necessary before we can make a decision, and so we sensibly make up our minds on broad considerations, drawn from the state of the case.

Of course, reliance upon this habit of mind may mislead us: 'it is scarcely necessary to point out how much our inclinations have to do with our belief.' Again, ' "Trifles light as air" are all that the predisposed mind requires for belief and action.' And so, when we rely on probabilities which do not exist, 'or

our wishes are inordinate, or our opinions are wrong, our Faith
degenerates into weakness, extravagance, superstition, enthusiasm, bigotry, prejudice, as the case may be; but when our
prepossessions are unexceptionable, then we are right in
believing or not believing, not indeed without, but upon
slender evidence.'

Thus Faith is a moral principle:

it is created in the mind, not so much by facts, as by probabilities; and since probabilities have no definite ascertained value, and are reducible to no scientific standard,
what are such to each individual, depends on his moral
temperament. A good and a bad man will think very
different things probable. In the judgment of a rightly
disposed mind, objects are desirable and attainable which
irreligious men will consider to be but fancies.

At this point, the careless reader may feel that Newman
has been guilty of tautology, and that he has said no more
than that the religious man takes to religion, while the irreligious man does not, and that both are more or less born into
their respective states of mind, a doctrine which looks suspi-
ciously deterministic.

Such a line of thought would overlook Newman's starting-
point, the creature's need of the Creator. The conscience,
man's insufficiency, and desire for a God should dispose the
mind towards feeling that a Revelation is probable, and hence
the mind will accept the proof of a Revelation which is brought
before it. The will's task is to heed the promptings of the
conscience and the desire for the existence of a God, and to
act upon them; whether a man feels that a Revelation is
probable or not depends on the way he lives his life. In this
way Newman is able to say that a man is either religiously
or irreligiously disposed without running the danger of determinism.

But it might be urged that although Newman's theory
can be successfully defended against the charge of determinism,
it is still open to the objection that education or environ-
mental influence will as effectively determine a man's religious-
ness as Divine determinism. Newman would probably meet
this criticism by asserting that it is our affair whether we live

our lives according to broad criteria of good and bad, and for the rest, would probably accept the point that our environment can decisively affect our beliefs: 'Habit, formation of mind, prejudice, reliance and faith in others, may be as real walls of separation as mountains.'[46] Thus he would contemplate a large category of those whose invincible ignorance is complete, and whose habits and prejudices are such that they cannot possibly be made to change their ways.

Some hints may be gleaned here of the ultimate motives and reasons for belief in God, and these will be considered in due course; in the interim, we shall discuss three instances of Newman's deployment of the Argument from Antecedent Probability.

First, we take an example from the *Via Media*, which is remarkable in that Newman escapes the force of his antecedent probability. In the lecture on the indefectibility of the Church Catholic, he takes issue with the Roman Catholic claim that their Church 'is pure and spotless in all matters great and small, that she can never decide wrongly on any point of faith and morals, but in every age possesses and teaches explicitly, or implicitly, the whole truth. . . .'[47] Newman grants that he sees no antecedent reason why a fulfilment of the prophecy should not have been intended, 'though it has not taken place'. As an apologist for the Anglican Church, of course, he could not allow that what might antecedently have been expected had historically taken place, and so he proceeds to evolve a closely argued mesh in order to escape his own probability. He points out that it is more modest to put only a general sense on the words of the promise, and then has to admit again that 'there surely is no antecedent reason why Almighty God should not have designed to bestow on the Church that perfect purity which the Roman Church claims for her.' Next he shows that throughout the inspired history there are traces of divine intentions mysteriously frustrated, and so he argues that the Christian Church has forfeited a portion of the promises by breaking the condition of Unity, which explains why the event has not fulfilled the expectation.[48]

Thus when Newman became a Roman Catholic, he had only to brush away his careful arguments, to leave a broad intelli-

[46] *L. and D.* xx. 269.   [47] *V.M.* i. 196.   [48] *V. M.* i. 199.

gible antecedent probability, a perception 'that on the whole facts point to certain definite conclusions, and not to their contraries',[49] operating in favour of the Roman Catholic Church. In other words, the fundamental trend of his mind, the abstract recognition of the possibility that a Church could be pure, was the same whether he was an Anglican or a Roman Catholic. The necessities of the Anglican system demanded, however, that he argue against this trend, and so evidently this is another case when we can say that Roman Catholicism was more *natural* to him than Anglicanism.

Arguments *a priori* and *a posteriori* are the twin pillars upon which the *Essay on the Development of Christian Doctrine* is founded. We have already remarked that the principle of reserve is the essence of development, in that the Church gradually discloses what had lain hidden and implicit in its bosom; now we see that the argument from antecedent probability is the means whereby Newman advances from what we know to what we wish to know, from the explicit portion of Revelation to the implicit portion. Thus in the second chapter 'On the antecedent argument in behalf of developments in Christian doctrine', Newman addresses himself to the task of showing that developments of doctrine are to be expected.

Newman derives this expectation from the form of the Bible: 'Since then Scripture needs completion, the question is brought to this issue, whether defect or inchoateness in its doctrines be or be not an antecedent probability in favour of a development of them.'[50]

Next he argues from the analogy of nature, pointing out that 'in whatever sense the need and its supply are a proof of design in the visible creation, in the same do the gaps, if the word may be used, which occur in the structure of the original creed of the Church, make it probable that those developments, which grow out of the truths which lie around it, were intended to fill them up.'[51]

Further, Newman notes the progressive nature of Revelation, arguing that if 'the prophetic sentences have had that development which has really been given them, first by succeeding revelations, and then by the event, it is probable antecedently that those doctrinal, political, ritual, and ethical

[49] *V.M.* i. 109.   [50] *Dev.* 62.   [51] *Dev.* 63.

sentences, which have the same structure, should admit the same expansion'.[52]

Hence Newman is able to proceed to a second section, titled 'An infallible Authority to be expected', with the conclusion:

> It has now been made probable that developments of Christianity were but natural, as time went on, and were to be expected; and that these natural and true developments, as being natural and true, were of course contemplated and taken into account by its Author, who in designing the work designed its legitimate results. (*Dev.* 75)

The next question is to ascertain the developments which are legitimate, leading in turn to the need for an authority to sanction these developments. Newman argues the probability of such an authority in the same way as he had argued the probability of developments:

> Let the state of the case be carefully considered. If the Christian doctrine, as originally taught, admits of true and important developments, as was argued in the foregoing Section, this is a strong antecedent argument in favour of a provision in the Dispensation for putting a seal of authority upon those developments. (*Dev.* 79)

For Newman, the fact that an authority *exists*, and the fact that an authority is *needed*, are strikingly coincidental: 'the absolute need of a spiritual supremacy is at present the strongest of arguments in favour of the fact of its supply.' And in the same way, Newman argues in the third section that the existing developments of doctrine are the probable fulfilment of the expectation.

In his section on the 'State of the Evidence', Newman defends this approach from criticisms which might be urged from the Baconian school of logic. Essentially, he argues that in some subjects there is no other approach, that 'we must be content to follow the law of our being in religious matters as well as in secular',[53] and finally, that God will safeguard such a method: 'The less exact methods of reasoning may do

---

[52] *Dev.* 66.   [53] *Dev.* 115.

His work as well as the more perfect, if He blesses them. He may bless antecedent probabilities in ethical inquiries, who blesses experience and induction in the art of medicine.'[54] Newman then passes from the argument *a priori* to *a posteriori*, and offers instances to prove that expectations of developments have been legitimately fulfilled.

The final part of the book, applying seven tests to establish that developments are legitimate, has perhaps caused the most difficulty of comprehension; Owen Chadwick, for example, commented dismissively that Newman alleged the tests 'half-heartedly'.[55] The mistake here is to view the tests as separate from the body of proof, when in fact they are complementary; we should notice that the seven tests represent the same method of reasoning employed throughout the Essay. Newman is saying that the Primitive Church exhibits marked characteristics, and that it would only be reasonable to expect that a later Church which preserved the essence of the earlier Church should manifest these same characteristics. The crucial question then, is this: Has the expectation been borne out by the event? And of course, for Newman it has.

Although the tests seem inclusive of developments rather than exclusive, they serve to determine the limits available for development by pointing to the scope which had been left by the Primitive Church. Just as a farmer may buy and fence a very large tract of land, but only cultivate part of it, leaving it for his descendants to bring the rest under cultivation, so Newman conceives that the Church has grown to fill out the pattern afforded by the early Church. Hence when J. B. Mozley attacked him for asserting that 'Whatever is is right',[56] that all developments are legitimate, and that Newman had only considered the decay of ideas rather than the extravagance, Newman would have replied that he had given 'the *rules* which keep it [development] from extravagating endlessly'.[57] Further, he would have maintained that in modern times doctrines which were explicit were coterminous

---

[54] *Dev.* 111.

[55] Owen Chadwick, *From Bossuet to Newman: The Idea of Doctrinal Development*, Cambridge, 1957, p. 155.

[56] J. B. Mozley, *The Theory of Development. A Criticism of Dr. Newman's Essay on the Development of Christian Doctrine*, London, 1878, p. 118.

[57] *L. and D.* xx. 54.

with doctrines which had remained implicit in the Primitive Church: 'I should hold that *the substance* of the res credenda or dogma of Christianity was just what it was in the Apostle's day—and that the difference between the creed then and the creed now, was only quoad nos—or of *apprehension*.'[58]

The *Essay on the Development of Christian Doctrine* therefore offers the most extensive use of antecedent probability ever made by Newman, and it is timely to make some comments on the usefulness of the argument. Its effectiveness depends on the rigour with which it is applied and expressed by its author, for if the probability is put too high, then the reader will not be carried along, and the object of the argument is defeated. As the example from the *Via Media* has shown, Newman felt and expressed the force of each argument from antecedent probability with conspicuous fairness.

Its effect upon the reader depends also on the homogeneity of phenomena. If a particular order of events in the past gives rise to a certain expectation, we have to be reasonably sure that the same relationship between events will continue to hold good at other times and in other circumstances.

Further, we have to feel that phenomena are unlikely to deceive us, and that events which seem natural, probable, and inevitable are not going to be frustrated during the course of history. For this assurance, one needs to feel with Newman that if this process of reasoning is to lead to God, then God is unlikely to deceive.

It is worth remarking, too, that one judges better of probabilities if one has experience of the subject. The inexperienced reader who follows Newman's assessment of the strength of certain probabilities may be led astray, but this still proves that he is willing to embrace the same conclusions that Newman has reached.

Newman would probably meet these comments with remarks such as '. . . the general impressions of conscientious men are true ones',[59] or '. . . the experience of life contains abundant evidence that in practical matters, when their minds are really roused, men commonly are not bad reasoners.'[60] The argument from antecedent probability offers an excellent

---

[58] *L. and D.* xx. 224.   [59] *Ess.* ii. 367.
[60] *U.S.* 211: 13 January 1839.

opportunity of giving a fair appraisal of the strength of the case, clears away prejudice, and provides a logical method which, though not syllogistically logical, is still methodical.

The third example, drawn from the *Grammar of Assent*, shows how, almost half a century after Newman adopted the argument from Whately, the approach is invaluable in its clarity and persuasiveness.

Once Newman has founded Natural Religion upon the Conscience, he proceeds to argue that there is a presumption that a Revelation will be given:

> One of the most important effects of Natural Religion on the mind, in preparation for Revealed, is the anticipation which it creates, that a Revelation will be given. That earnest desire of it, which religious minds cherish, leads the way to the expectation of it. . . . This presentiment is founded on our sense, on the one hand, of the infinite goodness of God, and, on the other, of our own extreme misery and need—two doctrines which are the primary constituents of Natural Religion. It is difficult to put a limit to the legitimate force of this antecedent probability. Some minds will feel it to be so powerful, as to recognize in it almost a proof, without direct evidence, of the divinity of a religion claiming to be the true, supposing its history and doctrine are free from positive objection, and there be no rival religion with plausible claims of its own. (*G.A.* 422 f.)

Then, after the argument *a priori*, comes the argument *a posteriori*: 'Now as to the fact; has what is so probable in anticipation actually been granted to us, or have we still to look out for it?'[61]

This line of reasoning helps to elucidate a remark made by Newman in a letter, that he felt the logical proof for the being of a Revelation was far stronger than the logical proof for the being of a God.[62] If we take up this train of thought, we find that the same sort of antecedent considerations prevail in Newman's ideas as to the proof of God's existence. It was a maxim of Newman's that supply creates a demand, that journals create their own readers and teachers their own

[61] *G.A.* 429.   [62] *L. and D.* xv. 457.

hearers,[63] and it will be noted from a previous quotation that Newman also talked there in terms of supply and demand; he conceived that the notion that God exists, and the wish for Him to exist, both imply His existence. This is brought out clearly in *Callista*, when Caecilius says:

> . . . if all your thoughts go one way; if you have needs, desires, aims, aspirations, all of which demand an Object, and imply, by their very existence, that such an Object does exist also; and if nothing here does satisfy them, and if there be a message which professes to come from that Object, of whom you already have the presentiment, and to teach you about Him, and to bring the remedy you crave; and if those who try that remedy say with one voice that the remedy answers; are you not bound, Callista, at least to look that way, to inquire into what you hear about it, and to ask for His help, if He be, to enable you to believe in Him?[64]

Again we find the twin argument of expectation and event, but the method proved capable of even greater refinement and simplicity, in this letter of 1884 to Wilfrid Ward:

> As to the matter and main argument of your Essay, it seems to me you mean to say that the same considerations which make you wish to believe are among the reasons which, when you actually do inquire, *lead you prudently* to believe, thus serving a double purpose. Do you bring this out anywhere? On the contrary, are you not shy of calling those considerations reasons? Why? (Ward ii. 489)

Thus, in the end, a method of reasoning adopted in the Oriel Common Room, is presented in its final, unassailable form. One believes because one wishes to believe; that one believes, implies that one is right to believe. Newman had always maintained that it was impossible to argue a man into belief, and now, simply stated, his duty was to declare that man's desire for God's existence correlated His existence.

---

[63] Cf. *H.S.* i. 165: '. . . a great school lived in demand and supply, and . . . the supply must be before the demand.'

[64] *Callista, A Sketch of the Third Century*, London, 1873, p. 220.

IV. APPLICATIONS OF THE PRINCIPLE TO A NUMBER OF TOPICS

The principle of reserve is one of measure and discrimination; it withholds knowledge until it perceives a real desire and need for the knowledge it possesses. But it need not be knowledge that should be reserved; the same principle can be discerned at work in Newman's feelings about the exercise of power and authority. In a letter, he wrote: 'I have never got over the Rambler being taken out of my hands, and I do not think I shall; not, I trust, from any resentful and other similar feeling, but it has been the same shock to my nerves that a pat from a lion would be. Great powers ought not lightly to be brought into exercise . . .'[65] The same feeling evidently prompted the comment to Bellasis, that 'you lawyers are far too powerful a gun not to be reserved for some great occasion.'[66]

Newman's theories on various topics are derived from the principle of reserve; his journalistic theory, for example, is that one should reserve fire in order to make it more telling. Speaking of the *Rambler*, he told Acton that it should adopt the policy of Wellington in the lines of Torres Vedras, and keep within shelter, watching the enemy so as to be able to take him at a disadvantage:

> Let it go back to its own literary line. Let it be instructive, clever, and amusing. Let it cultivate a general temper of good humour and courtesy. Let it praise as many persons as it can, and gain friends in neutral quarters, and become the organ of others by the interest it has made them take in its proceedings. Then it will be able to plant a good blow at a fitting time with great effect . . . Power to be powerful, and strength, to be strong, must be exerted only now and then. (*L. and D.* xviii. 562)

More important, the principle of reserve is to be seen at work behind Newman's ecclesiastical theory:

> I will tell you what seems to me the real grievance: viz. that in this generation, the Bishops should pass such grave

[65] *L. and D.* xxi. 23.   [66] *K.C.* 183.

matters (to use the Oxford term) by *cumulation*. The wisdom of the Church has provided many courts for theological questions, one higher than another, and with an appeal from the lower to the higher. I suppose, in the middle ages, which had a manliness and boldness of which there is now so great a lack, a question was first debated in a University; then in one University against another; or by one order of friars against another; then perhaps it came before a theological faculty; then it went to the metropolitan; and so by various stages and after many examinations and judgments, it came before the Holy See. But now what do the Bishops do? All courts are superseded, because the whole English-speaking Catholic population all over the world is under Propaganda, an arbitrary, military power. Propaganda is our only court of appeal; but to it the Bishops go, and secure it and commit it, before they move one step in the matter which calls for interference. And how is Propaganda to know anything about an English controversy, since it talks Italian? . . .

Meanwhile, it is a grave consideration, that in England, as things are, upon theological questions the Pope and the individual Catholic meet each other face to face, without media for collision, without the safeguard of springs or cushions, with a jar; and the quasi-military power of Propaganda has the jurisdiction and the control of the intellect. (*L. and D.* xx. 391 f.) [67]

Newman anticipates the same effects from the use of naked power that he anticipated from the disclosure of complete knowledge; he feels that knowledge and power should be transmitted through media which qualify them and render them suitable for the recipient. This was an application of the principle of reserve which he only learned through hard experience, when he was consistently misunderstood by his superiors. He expresses the frustration of having no barrier to absorb the shock of authority when, after much the same argument as above, he writes: '*Now*, if I, as a private priest,

---

[67] Cf. *Apo.* 231: ' "O, it is excellent," says the poet, "to have a giant's strength, but tyrannous, to use it like a giant." I think history supplies us with instances in the Church, where legitimate power has been harshly used.'

put anything into print, *Propaganda* answers me at once. How can I fight with such a chain on my arm? It is like the Persians driven on to fight *under the lash*.'[68] He uses the same imagery of springs and cushions in his social theory, which is undoubtedly influenced by the principle of reserve, as may be seen from this fragment: '. . . . in the world society gets on, and a family gets on, by a refined system of mutual concession. Society is like a carriage going on springs, where every collision and jar is anticipated.'[69] Newman seems to feel that there must be spaces between each source of power, so that each has room to breathe and manœuvre. This leads to a theory of ecclesiastical detachment, the main theme of which is that the Holy See should rely upon its own genius, and keep itself detached from others. Newman spoke of detachment as a virtue in itself with warm approval; at one time he remarked: 'What a great thing it is to be independent or detached',[70] and starts in much the same way in the first volume of *Historical Sketches*; 'Detachment, as we know from spiritual books, is a rare and high Christian virtue; a great Saint, St Philip Neri, said that, if he had a dozen really detached men, he should be able to convert the world. To be detached is to be loosened from every tie which binds the soul to the earth, to be dependent on nothing sublunary, to lean on nothing temporal . . .'[71] Shortly afterwards, he gives an example of the way in which ecclesiastical detachment works; the Pope was advised to 'make sure of the coat-tail of Austria, and hold on'. Yet, although there was a close relationship between the Holy See and the Holy Roman Empire, the Pope did just the reverse: 'He made light of this master of political wisdom, and showed his independence of Austria;—not that he did not honour Austria, but that he honoured the Rock of Peter more. And what has been the consequence? he has simply gained by his fidelity to his position . . . Here is an instance of what I have called "ecclesiastical detachment", and of its working.'[72] This example is not particularly important in itself, but it has the virtue of prompting the mind to inquire how much is gained when one nation takes upon itself to interfere in the affairs of another nation.

[68] *L. and D.* xx. 447.   [69] *L. and D.* xv. 402.   [70] *L. and D.* xviii. 45.
[71] *H. S.* i. 130.   [72] *H.S.* i. 142.

One of the subjects which Newman touches upon frequently in the *Parochial Sermons* and elsewhere is 'excitement'. He has a horror of exciting the feelings for no purpose, and so tells us:

> God has made us feel in order that we may *go on to act* in consequence of feeling; if then we allow our feelings to be excited without acting upon them, (e.g. by reading a novel) we do mischief to the moral system within us, just as we might spoil a watch, or other piece of mechanism, by playing with the wheels of it. We weaken its springs, and they cease to act truly. (*P.S.* ii. 371: 18 October 1831)

Newman discloses his full meaning several pages later, when he writes:

> . . . I call all formal and intentional expression of religious emotions, all studied passionate discourse, *dissipation,*— dissipation the same in nature, though different in subject, as what is commonly so called; for it is a drain and a waste of our religious and moral strength, a general weakening of our spiritual powers (as I have already shown); and all for what? —for the pleasure of the immediate excitement. (*P.S.* ii. 377)

The use of the word 'dissipation' here shows that Newman conceives that there is only a certain stock or reservoir of religious feelings, which must be husbanded and measured out at the proper time. Those who seize all opportunities for reveal-ing their piety, and strain to rouse a devotional spirit within themselves, may gain temporarily, but in a short time will have exhausted their stock of higher feelings, and will then sink back to a lower state than they formerly occupied. Newman repeats this time and time again, in sermons and other works; he urges people never to act under excitement. Thus when Father Bernard was being expelled from the Oratory for his 'spiritual love' for Mrs. Wootten, Newman, from Abbotsford, where he was recuperating after the Achilli trial, entreated all parties to act with deliberation, and not to act 'under excitement'.[73]

In view of this, it is no surprise to find that Newman employs reserve as a fruitful principle in psychology, and frequently

[73] *L. and D.* xv. 257.

attributes reserve to men whose characters he depicts; Cicero, for example, was reserved. But the longest and most instructive of his characterizations involving reserve is that of Davison, which is worth quoting at length:

It will be recollected that we have been speaking of that economy of reserve and secrecy, to which our author seems to have been inclined, as other similar minds; and now we will point out another of its secondary causes, or, as they may be called, its phenomena. We mean the difficulty he seems to have had in expressing himself, and the consequent effort which, not only composition, but even conversation, or we may say speech, cost him, and the effect of this difficulty visible in his writings. . . .

We suppose it then to be undeniable, that there are persons, whose minds are full of thought even to bursting, in whom it is pent up in a strange way, and in whom, when it at last forces itself out in language, it does so with the suddenness, brevity, completeness, and effectiveness (if the comparison be allowed) of a steam-boiler. . . . Again, minds which vividly realize conclusions, often are irritated at the necessity of drawing out premises; or they are inadequate to the task; or they are impatient of many words; or they are at a loss where to begin; or they despair of conveying their meaning to others; or they find relief to their feelings in some sudden and strong outbreak. When, under such circumstances, there is a habit of self-government, and a watchful control of feeling and language, there will often be an abruptness of speech in consequence; or an unseasonable silence; or an uneasy patience, an unaccountable constraint, a composure without repose; or a variable jerking manner, as if a man were riding his horse with a tight rein. Or sometimes, to recur to our former figure, he will let off the steam in the shape of humour. Or when the mind feels its own separation from others, its strangeness, its isolation, a distance of demeanour in general society is the consequence, which apparently argues a want of frankness and cordiality, or a recklessness, which may be set down to arrogance and pride. All these mental states are destructive of ease of deportment; to which must be added what is sometimes

called *consciousness*, the painful perception of the presence
of self, quite distinct from self-importance and self-conceit,
though looking like them to undiscriminating eyes. (*Ess.*
ii. 380 ff.)

This portrait is one of a long line in which the principal feature
is reserve, and in which Newman exhibits his mastery of the
psychology of reserve. In the *Parochial Sermons* he writes of
religious men who are not understood by the world because
they are not of the world, so that 'even the better sort of men
are often disconcerted and vexed by them', because they act
upon very different principles from those which are commonly
taken for granted; they assume, 'as first principles, what the
world wishes to have proved in detail. They have become
familiar with the sights of the next world, till they talk of them
as if all men admitted them.' As a result, they cannot enter into
the ways in which other men think, and so they seem 'abrupt
in what they say and do; nay, even make others feel constrained
and uneasy in their presence. Perhaps they appear reserved too,
because they take so much for granted which might be drawn
out, and because they cannot bring themselves to tell all their
thoughts from their sacredness, and because they are. drawn
off from free conversation to the thought of heaven, on which
their minds rest.'[74]

Newman speaks with even greater decision in the *Sermons
on Subjects of the Day*: 'Religious men, on the contrary, are very
reserved, if only that they dare not betray, if we may so speak,
God's confidence.'[75] If God is hidden from us, so is the religious
man:

> But there are others who look just the same to the world,
> who in their hearts are very different; they make no great
> show, they go on in the same quiet ordinary way as the
> others, but really they are training to be saints in Heaven.
> They do all they can to change themselves, to become like
> God, to obey God, to discipline themselves, to renounce the
> world; but they do it in secret, both because God tells them
> so to do, and because they do not like it to be known. More-
> over, there are a number of others between these two with

---

[74] *P.S.* iv. 235: 10 December 1837.   [75] *S.D.* 353: 19 December 1841.

more or less of worldliness and more or less of faith. Yet they all look about the same, to common eyes, because true religion is a hidden life in the heart; and though it cannot exist without deeds, yet these are for the most part secret deeds, secret charities, secret prayers, secret self-denials, secret struggles, secret victories. (*P.S.* iv. 243: 25 December 1837)

And so we return, as seems always to be the case, to the heart of Newman's teaching, 'the thought of two and two only absolute and luminously self-evident beings, myself and my Creator';[76] religious men are reserved towards the world, because in fact the world scarcely exists for them; all that is left is themselves and God:

The foundations of the ocean, the vast realms of water which girdle the earth, are as tranquil and as silent in the storm as in a calm. So is it with the souls of holy men. They have a well of peace springing up within them unfathomable; and though the accidents of the hour may make them seem agitated, yet in their hearts they are not so.

. . . For, as I have said, the Christian has a deep, silent, hidden peace, which the world sees not,—like some well in a retired and shady place, difficult of access. He is the greater part of his time by himself, and when he is in solitude, that is his real state. What he is when left to himself and to his God, that is his true life. He can bear himself; he can (as it were) joy in himself, for it is the grace of God within him, it is the presence of the Eternal Comforter, in which he joys. (*P.S.* v. 69: 22 December 1839)

[76] *Apo.* 18.

CHAPTER FIVE

RESERVE AS A STATE OF MIND—
SPECULATIONS ON NEWMAN'S
CHARACTER

So many and so varied are the manifestations of reserve which have been discussed, that it seems likely that a distinctive cast of mind is responsible for them all. The fundamental perception of this cast of mind is that this world is insufficient, and that the real world lies somewhere else. Newman expresses this in the *Parochial Sermons* when he writes:

> . . . this is the case on all sides of us; the outward world is found not to be enough for man, and he looks for some refuge near him, more intimate, more secret, more pure, more calm and stable. This is a main reason and a praiseworthy one, why a great number of the better sort of men look forward to marriage as the great object of life. They call it being settled, and so it is. The mind finds nothing to satisfy it in the employments and amusements of life, in its excitements, struggles, anxieties, efforts, aims, and victories. (*P.S.* iv. 188 f.: 22 October 1837)

Clearly, the mind which finds the physical world insufficient will be receptive to clues pointing towards a greater fulfilment than it can find in its own world; it will be anxious to find something which can complete its own incomplete world. And so one who possesses this type of mind will come to regard the world as a veil, and will try to pierce beyond its apparently consistent series of causes and effects to the real laws beyond, which are the laws of Providence:

> This is the law of Providence here below; it works beneath a veil, and what is visible in its course does but shadow out at most, and sometimes obscures and disguises what is invisible. The world in which we are placed has its own system of laws and principles, which, as far as our own know-

ledge of it goes, is, when once set in motion, sufficient to account for itself,—as complete and independent as if there was nothing beyond it. Ordinarily speaking, nothing happens, nothing goes on in the world, but may be satisfactorily traced to some other event or fact in it, or has a sufficient result in other events or facts in it, without the necessity of our following it into a higher system of things in order to explain its existence, or to give it a meaning. We will not stop to dwell on exceptions to this general statement, or on the narrowness of our knowledge of things: but what is every day said and acted on proves that this is at least the impression made upon most minds by the course of things in which we find ourselves. The sun rises and sets on a law; the tides ebb and flow upon a law; the earth is covered with verdure or buried in the ocean, it grows old and it grows young again, by the operation of fixed laws. Life, whether vegetable or animal, is subjected to a similar external and general rule. Men grow to maturity, then decay and die. Moreover, they form into society, and society has its principles. Nations move forward by laws which act as a kind of destiny over them, and which are as vigorous now as a thousand years ago. And these laws of the social and political world run into the physical, making all that is seen one and one only system; a horse stumbles, and an oppressed people is rid of their tyrant; a volcano changes populous cities into a dull lake; a gorge has of old time opened, and the river rolls on, bearing on its bosom the destined site of some great mart, which else had never been. We cannot set limits either to the extent or to the minuteness of this wonderful web of causes and effects, in which all we see is involved. It reaches to the skies; it penetrates into our very thoughts, habits, and will. . . .

What is called and seems to be cause and effect, is rather an order of sequence, and does not preclude, nay, perhaps implies, the presence of unseen spiritual agency as its real author. This is the animating principle both of the Church's ritual and of Scripture interpretation; in the latter it is the basis of the theory of the double sense; in the former it makes ceremonies and observances to be signs, seals, means, and pledges of supernatural grace. It is the mystical principle in the one, it is the sacramental in the other. All that is seen,—the world, the Bible, the Church, the civil polity, and man himself,—are types, and, in their degree and place, representatives and organs of an unseen world, truer and higher than themselves. (*Ess.* ii. 190 ff.)

More than anything, this remarkable passage convinces us of Newman's ever-abiding sense of the possibilities and depths existing in objects which to a person of duller perceptions might seem merely solid; he was able to discount appearances, and to pierce beneath, beyond the apparently consistent physical laws to the laws of Providence.

Undoubtedly this view of the material world springs from his scepticism. Speaking of the passage in the *Arians* where he says that the mind 'seems to itself at the moment to have cut all the ties which bind it to the universe, and to be floated off upon the ocean of interminable scepticism',[1] he writes in the Letters: 'I would say that this sense of God's presence is the only protection (which I have had to keep me from unlimited scepticism, though an overabundantly sufficient one) and that I expressed it in the first book I wrote . . .'[2] This scepticism led him to regard the material world as unreal and insufficient, and to feel that the real world was somewhere else, where it was hidden from him.

Thus we may attribute the way in which Newman habitually and naturally employs the principle of reserve from his earliest days to his possession of a type of mind which cannot be content with what appears on the surface, and which must continually strive after a reality elsewhere. But it is necessary to go further, and to ask what effect this type of mind has on character and characteristics.

Such effects are plainly discernible in his behaviour; he himself noted that:

All my life I have complained of ἀδυναμία [powerlessness], as I have called it. I mean a strange imprisonment, as if a chain were round my limbs and my faculties, hindering me doing more than a certain maximum—a sort of moral tether. People have said 'Why don't you *speak* louder?

[1] *Ari.* 76.   [2] *L. and D.* xviii. 335.

You speak, as far as you go, with such evident ease, you certainly can do more if you wish and try—' I can only answer, 'I can't'. I am kept in my circle by my moral tether, which pulls me up abruptly. (*L. and D.* xv. 242)[3]

We would hesitate to take this statement at its face value, did he not say much the same thing at other times, which have already been quoted in the first chapter. These statements thus acquire a cumulative force, which makes it certain that Newman was conscious that the principle of reserve was being applied to himself, and that he was restrained from exercising his full powers, in speaking or in anything else.

Similarly, other remarks he makes about himself may be only the chance remark of a moment, or they may be truths about himself of which he had slowly become conscious. Thus when he says: 'What seems indecision or obscurity in me is but the expression of a habit of *gradualness*',[4] the word 'gradualness' may be a reference to the gradations in which knowledge is disclosed and pursued, or it may merely mean that he is cautious. At other times, it is equally possible that what is really caution may be attributed to reserve, as when he asks his correspondent to 'excuse me, if, from an habitual reluctance to give my opinion, I seemed to be reserved.'[5]

To attempt a summary of Newman's behaviour, it seems certain that he was felt to be reserved in manner, if we can judge from this letter of Acton's:

> I had a three hours' talk with the venerable Noggs who came out at last with his real sentiments to an extent which startled me, with respect both to things and persons, as HE, Ward, Dalgairns, etc., etc., natural inclination of men in power to tyrannize, ignorance and presumption of our would-be theologians, in short what you and I would comfortably say over a glass of whiskey. I did not think he could ever cast aside his diplomacy and buttonment so entirely . . . (*L. and D.* xviii. 559 n.3)

---

[3] Cf. also *A.W.* 82: '. . . being in a way incapable, as if physically, of enthusiasm, however legitimate and guarded . . .' Cf. also *A.W.* 248: '. . . in the movement of my affections, . . . my physical strength cannot go beyond certain limits.'

[4] *L. and D.* xiv. 277.

[5] *L. and D.* xix. 291.

Of course, this is unjust. Placed as he was, Newman was forced to be reserved in his communications. He was critical of the way things were going, and he was out of favour with authority, and so reserve was his only resource. Yet this passage does underline the fact that Newman experienced some constraint in his dealings with others. He himself attributed this to shyness, while other people might, and did, attribute it to reserve or diplomacy. The time when Newman was reduced to writing a note to another member of the Oratory, because he was too shy to speak to him emphasizes the important point that Newman was highly aware of himself as a unique and separate consciousness, cut off from anyone else.[6] And so he writes of himself to his mother in 1836: 'I am not more lonely than I have been a long while. God intends me to be lonely; He has so framed my mind that I am in a great measure beyond the sympathies of other people and thrown upon Himself.'[7] It is possible that this is sheer bravado, and that he is doing no more than fabricating a theory to explain loneliness; however, much later, after Capes had written a perceptive review of the *Dream of Gerontius*, Newman wrote to him that 'I have often been puzzled at myself, that I should be both particularly fond of being alone, and particularly fond of being with friends. . . .'[8] So aware is Newman of the distance which separates one mind from another, and of the difficulties of understanding, that he is *self-conscious*, a fact which he notes in the autobiographical memoir prefixed to the volumes of Anglican letters: 'This untowardness in him was increased by a vivid selfconsciousness, which sometimes inflicted on him days of acute suffering from the recollection of solecisms, whether actual or imagined, which he recognized in his conduct in society.'[9] It may be recollected that in the character-sketch of Davison, Newman speaks of his reserve and self-consciousness, which seem to run together. Thus we may conjecture that the sense that everything is hidden from him drives Newman back into himself, and renders him shy and self-conscious. Curiously enough, this may explain why Newman is so preoccupied with

[6] Cf. *L. and D.* xiii. 28: 'You must make allowances for me, and bear with me, My dear F.A., for I am a shy person, and what that is, only shy persons know.'
[7] Moz. ii. 197.   [8] *L. and D.* xxiv. 53.
[9] *A.W.* 65.

himself, in his letters to his friends, and why he analyses himself and his actions at such length.

The principle of reserve entails an understanding of distinctions and gradations, for if a person has the duty of communicating knowledge, he must be able to perceive the differences which cause one piece of knowledge to be communicated, while another is reserved. Thus this type of mind is capable of nice distinctions, and fine discriminations, and so is best summed up in the words subtlety and sensitivity. It is plain that Newman possesses all these characteristics; he makes fine distinctions, such as his defence of the word 'dreary' to describe Anglican services,[10] and places great weight on words such as 'might' in the controversy with the London Oratory.[11] Further, his possession of this type of mind explains why Newman attempted such great precision in his writings, for if one is catering for a particular mentality, then writings must be adjusted to fit that mentality with exactitude. Hence, Newman protested that his lectures, which were published as the *Idea of a University*, might be 'from beginning to end a failure—from my not knowing my audience'.[12] But more important still, he whose task it is to disclose knowledge has to be acutely sensitive to the needs of the person who will receive the knowledge. Thus it is a laborious task, and so Newman wrote 'I have hardly written anything, unless I was *called* to do so',[13] and Mrs Froude said that 'other Catholics always seemed "making a case" when they said things to me,—*you* always contrived to say exactly what suited my mind.'[14] This testimony is borne out many times in Newman's correspondence, particularly with Robert and Henry Wilberforce, and helps to explain how Newman gained such great influence over the young men of Oxford.

Another tendency of the mind to which reserve is constitutional is its tendency to moderation and caution. For Newman, this aspect is perhaps best summed up in his maxim, 'Libertas in dubiis'. Thus he wrote: 'Catholics allow each other, accordingly, the greatest licence, and are, if I may so speak, utter *liberals*, as regards devotions, whereas they are most sensitive about doctrine.'[15] Similarly Newman asked Fisher if there was

[10] *L. and D.* xx. 339.   [11] *L. and D.* xviii. 176.   [12] *L. and D.* xv. 67.
[13] *L. and D.* xx. 169.   [14] *L. and D.* xvii. 544 n.2.   [15] *L. and D.* xvi. 341.

finality in his suggestions, and said: 'no one can religiously speak of development, without giving the *rules* which keep it from extravagating endlessly.'[16] It is interesting to note that the same principle prompts both of these diverse statements; in the first, moderation acts in the direction of toleration, while in the second, it acts as a minimizing influence. In both cases the influence of the principle of reserve is felt, refraining from the unnecessary exercise of authority, and keeping guard against excesses.

To conclude this description of the characteristics which belong to the type of mind which feels strongly that hidden reality lies elsewhere, it may be observed that the doctrine of original sin is particularly congenial to it, for if ignorance is one of the four penal wounds resulting from the Fall, then the fact that knowledge is reserved from the human race is the direct result of its own actions. Newman makes this causal relationship clear, when he writes:

> Let it be recollected that a mystery in religion is not a real thing *in rerum natura*, not anything objective, but something subjective. It presupposes a particular intellect contemplating facts or truths, and it is an incidence of the imperfection of that given intellect; and, as regards the race of man, it is in great measure the effect of that penal ignorance which is one of the four characteristics of our fallen state. (*L. and D.* xix. 532)[17]

Thus the very fact that knowledge is withheld from us will always warn us that the human race is sinful, and that the whole world is in the position which Newman took as the basis for a correspondence with Allies, 'Mundus totus in maligno positus est.'[18] This approach enables Newman to give a more satisfactory explanation of the question of evil:

> What has been most congenial to my own mind, is, to consider the beginnings of evil involved in the very idea of creation—though this of course is only throwing the difficulty a step back. The creature *must* be imperfect in itself—

---

[16] *L. and D.* xx. 54.

[17] The four characteristics are ignorance, malice, weakness, and concupiscence; see *Summa Theologiae*, ed. by T. Gilby, O.P., 1964, xxvi. 91.

[18] *L. and D.* xix. 421, 430.

the question is whether *imperfection* is not a *kind* of evil—
and then we go on to the different kind of evils, and the
certainty or chance of their resulting. (*L. and D.* xix. 212)

If we are in ignorance, and if reserve or an economical representation is employed towards ourselves, then we should
be aware that this method is an *expedient*—the best available,
but still not ideal. It is perhaps for this reason that Newman
combined awe at the 'terrible aboriginal calamity'[19] in which
the human race is implicated with gratitude for the kindly
expedients which God employed towards those who committed
such a crime. Hence we find him asking Gladstone to fulfil
his promise of some remarks on our Lord's method of teaching,
since 'it would be a great point, if from any source you could
find traces in His or His disciples' words, not of their purpose of
illuminating gradually, and their general recognition of its
necessity, but of the defects in the patterns of human perfection
which existed in the world, and made it necessary.'[20]

The final question which remains to be answered is how the
mind, once it has apprehended divine truths or mysteries, is to
'hold' these truths, and to make them real to itself. Truth
is an elusive thing, and recedes as we try to grasp it; even
if we grasp it, we find too often that we merely hold its husk,
and that its energizing power is dead. Newman recognized
that familiarity with an object or truth robs it of the mystery
and force it possesses when it is unknown:

And in such instances of certitude, the previous labour of
coming to a conclusion, and that repose of mind which I
have above described as attendant on an assent to its truth,
often counteracts whatever of lively sensation the fact thus
concluded is in itself adapted to excite; so that what is gained
in depth and exactness of belief is lost as regards freshness
and vigour. (*G.A.* 215)

When Newman urged his hearers to bring things home to
themselves, the danger was that truths would be tamed and so
lose the significance they once possessed by being external to
the mind. To use a maxim of Proust's, those truths would be

[19] *Apo.* 218.   [20] *L. and D.* xxiv. 8.

'like everything that is realised, sterilising'.[21] Possibly the use of the past tense in 'realised' may give a hint of how Newman solved this difficulty; the mind should constantly attempt to realize the unknown to itself, to make it its own, and to act upon it. It is not a process which is done and finished, but which is continuously being carried out; realizing enables one to grasp the mysterious, without being deprived of the mystery. Evidence for this view can be found in the *Grammar of Assent*:

> What is the peculiarity of our nature, in contrast with the inferior animals around us? It is that, though man cannot change what he is born with, he is a being of progress with relation to his perfection and characteristic good. Other beings are complete from their first existence, in that line of excellence which is allotted to them; but man begins with nothing realized (to use the word), and he has to make capital for himself by the exercise of those faculties which are his natural inheritance. Thus he gradually advances to the fulness of his original destiny. Nor is this process mechanical, nor is it of necessity; it is committed to the personal efforts of each individual of the species; each of us has the prerogative of completing his inchoate and rudimental nature, and of developing his own perfection out of the living elements with which his mind began to be. (*G.A.* 348 f.)

Throughout his life, man makes his own, 'realizes' what lies external to him. But Newman does not want ideas or beliefs to be laid up within one, so that they become formalized and forgotten; instead, the mind is to keep in touch with them as external to itself, so that one grasps them without becoming familiar with them. We find an example in the *Sermons* when Newman elucidates St. Paul's doctrine of justifying faith: '. . . he continues, "Now faith is the substance," that is, the realizing, "of things hoped for, the evidence," that is, the ground of proof, "of things not seen." It is in very essence the making present what is unseen . . . '[22] This is the reason why, as has often been noted, the words 'real', 'reality', and 'realize' occur so frequently in Newman's writings. Whenever he uses

[21] Marcel Proust, *Remembrance of Things Past*, tr. by C. K. Scott Moncrieff, London, 1966, iii. 341.
[22] *P.S.* iv. 296 f.: 21 February 1836.

these words, he may be thinking that the human mind loses essences by trying to possess them; that, as soon as it attempts to hold a truth firmly within its grasp, the truth evaporates and vanishes. His method ensures that novelty and mystery are retained even while a truth is held by the mind. The constant process of realization links the still-mysterious unknown with the realized known, so that the unknown does not lose its energizing power when it is assimilated into the mind. Life becomes permeated with the apprehension of the unseen, and a synthesis is formed between the material world and the unknown world beyond. This idea is never fully drawn out in Newman's writings; the nearest he comes to making it explicit is in the passage already quoted. Nevertheless, it is implicit in his life and works, and follows logically from the line of inquiry which has been pursued.

BIBLIOGRAPHY

I. MANUSCRIPT SOURCES

Birmingham Oratory, Newman Archives
Bodleian Library, Wilberforce Papers, C5
Cambridge University Library, Add. 7349

II. PRINTED SOURCES

i. J. H. NEWMAN

Apologia pro Vita Sua, ed. by M. J. Svaglic, Clarendon Press, Oxford, 1967

The Arians of the Fourth Century, Rivingtons, London, 1876

Autobiographical Writings, ed. by H. Tristram, Sheed & Ward, London, 1956

Callista, A Sketch of the Third Century, Burns, Oates & Co., London, 1873

Certain Difficulties felt by Anglicans in Catholic Teaching, 2 vols., vol. i, Burns, Oates & Co., London, 1872, vol. ii, Basil Montagu Pickering, London, 1876

Correspondence of John Henry Newman with John Keble and Others, 1839–45, ed. at the Birmingham Oratory, Longmans, London, 1917

An Essay in Aid of a Grammar of Assent, Burns, Oates & Co., London, 1881

An Essay on the Development of Christian Doctrine, London, 1876

Essays Critical and Historical, 2 vols., Basil Montagu Pickering, London, 1881

Fifteen Sermons preached before the University of Oxford, Rivingtons, London, 1872

Historical Sketches, 3 vols., Basil Montagu Pickering, London, 1872, 1873

Lectures on the Doctrine of Justification, Rivingtons, London, 1874

Lectures on the Present Position of Catholics in England, Burns, Oates & Co., London, 1880

Letters and Correspondence of John Henry Newman during his Life in the English Church, ed. by Anne Mozley, 2 vols., Longmans, London, 1891

The Letters and Diaries of John Henry Newman, ed. by C. S. Dessain, Oxford, 1961–, in progress

Parochial and Plain Sermons, ed. by W. J. Copeland, 8 vols., Rivingtons, London, 1868

The Philosophical Notebook of John Henry Newman, ed. by E. Sillem, Nauwelaerts, Louvain, 1970

Sermons bearing on Subjects of the Day, ed. by W. J. Copeland, London, 1869

The Via Media of the Anglican Church, 2 vols., London, 1877

WARD, WILFRID, *The Life of John Henry Cardinal Newman, based on his Private Journals and Correspondence*, 2 vols., Longmans, London, 1912

ii. CRITICAL, PATRISTIC, AND MISCELLANEOUS

ABBOTT, E. A. *The Anglican Career of Cardinal Newman*, 2 vols., Macmillan, London, 1892

AQUINAS, ST. THOMAS. *Summa Theologiae*, ed. by T. Gilby, O.P., Eyre & Spottiswoode, London, 1964

BEVERIDGE, W. *The Theological Works of William Beveridge*, 12 vols., J. H. Parker, Oxford, 1842–8

BREMOND, M. J. F. R. I. H. *The Mystery of Newman*, tr. by H. C. Corrance, Williams & Norgate, London, 1907

CHADWICK, W. O. *From Bossuet to Newman: The Idea of Doctrinal Development*, University Press, Cambridge, 1957

CLEMENT OF ALEXANDRIA. *The Writings of Clement of Alexandria*, tr. by the Revd. W. Wilson, 2 vols., Clark, Edinburgh, 1867, 1869

COPLESTON, E. *An Enquiry into the Doctrines of Necessity and Predestination. In Four Discourses preached before the University of Oxford*, London, 1821

DANIÉLOU, J. *Origen*, tr. by W. Mitchell, Sheed & Ward, London, 1955

DAVISON, J. *Discourses on Prophecy, in which are considered its Structure, Use, and Inspiration*, Murray, London, 1825

—— *The Remains and Occasional Publications of the late Rev. John Davison*, Oxford, 1841

HAWKINS, E. *A Dissertation upon the Use and Importance of Unauthoritative Tradition as an Introduction to the Christian Doctrines*, Oxford, 1819

—— *Systematic Preaching recommended in a Sermon preached June 4, 1825, in the Church of St Mary the Virgin, Oxford*, Oxford, 1825

JONES, OWAIN W. *Isaac Williams and his Circle*, London, 1971

MOZLEY, JOHN B. *The Theory of Development. A Criticism of Dr. Newman's Essay on the Development of Christian Doctrine*, Rivingtons, London, 1878

ORIGEN. *Origen. Contra Celsum*, tr. by H. Chadwick, University Press, Cambridge, 1953

PROTHERO, R. E. *The Life and Correspondence of Arthur Penrhyn Stanley, D. D.*, 2 vols., Murray, London, 1893

PROUST, M. *Remembrance of Things Past*, tr. by C. K. Scott Moncrieff, 12 vols., Chatto & Windus, London, 1966

SUMNER, JOHN B. *Apostolical Preaching considered in an Examination of St Paul's Epistles*, London, 1815

WHATELY, R. *Elements of Rhetoric. Comprising the Substance of an Article in the Encyclopaedia Metropolitana*, Oxford, 1828

—— *The Right Method of Interpreting Scripture, in what relates to the Nature of the Deity, and His Dealings with Mankind, illustrated, in a Discourse on Predestination by Dr. King, late Lord Archbishop of Dublin, preached at Christ Church, Dublin, before the House of Lords, May 15, 1709*, with notes by the Revd. Richard Whately, Oxford, 1821

WILLIAMS, ISAAC. *The Autobiography of Isaac Williams, B.D.*, ed. by the Ven. Sir George Prevost, Longmans, London, 1892

iii. PERIODICALS

MOZLEY, T. *British Critic and Quarterly Theological Review*, vol. xxxi, no. 61, 1842

NEWMAN, J. H. 'Duncan's Travels', *British Review and London Critical Journal*, vol. xxii, no 44, May 1824

NEWSOME, DAVID. 'Justification and Sanctification: Newman and the Evangelicals', *Journal of Theological Studies*, New Series, vol. xv, 1964

INDEX OF PERSONS

INDEX OF TOPICS